PUFFIN BOOKS

Editor: Kaye Webb

PS303

BY THE SHORES OF SILVER LAKE

This is the fourth story about Laura and her pioneering family. After living in a log cabin in the Wisconsin Woods and travelling West in a covered wagon to Minnesota, they were all longing for a home where Ma could unpack the china shepherdess for the very last time.

Pa wanted to settle in the new country in the West, so he accepted a job with a new railroad company, where he could look about for a homestead. Laura was enchanted by their first train journey, and the winter was spent in a house with an upstairs and glass windows.

They were snug and safe at Christmas that year, while the snow settled and the buffalo wolves prowled outside. And when spring came, and Pa had safely registered his claim to the homestead, they knew that all their adventures had been worth it.

If you want to catch up on the first three Laura books, *Little House in the Big Woods*, *Little House on the Prairie* and *On the Banks of Plum Creek* are all published in Puffins.

LAURA INGALLS WILDER

BY THE SHORES OF
SILVER LAKE

Illustrated by Garth Williams

PENGUIN BOOKS

Penguin Books Ltd, Harmondsworth, Middlesex, England
Penguin Books Australia Ltd, Ringwood, Victoria, Australia

—

First published in the U.S.A. 1939
Published in Great Britain by Lutterworth Press 1961
Published in Puffin Books 1967
Reprinted 1968

—

Text copyright © Harper & Bros., 1939
Pictures copyright © Garth Williams, 1953

—

Made and printed in Great Britain
by Richard Clay (The Chaucer Press) Ltd,
Bungay, Suffolk
Set in Monotype Plantin

CONTENTS

CHAPTER I

UNEXPECTED VISITOR

LAURA was washing the dishes one morning when old Jack, lying in the sunshine on the doorstep, growled to tell her that someone was coming. She looked out, and saw a buggy crossing the gravelly ford of Plum Creek.

'Ma,' she said, 'it's a strange woman coming.'

Ma sighed. She was ashamed of the untidy house, and so was Laura. But Ma was too weak and Laura was too tired and they were too sad to care very much.

Mary and Carrie and baby Grace and Ma had all had

scarlet fever. The Nelsons across the creek had had it too, so there had been no one to help Pa and Laura. The doctor had come every day; Pa did not know how he could pay the bill. Far worst of all, the fever had settled in Mary's eyes, and Mary was blind.

She was able to sit up now, wrapped in quilts in Ma's old hickory rocking-chair. All that long time, week after week, when she could still see a little, but less every day, she had never cried. Now she could not see even the brightest light any more. She was still patient and brave.

Her beautiful golden hair was gone. Pa had shaved it close because of the fever, and her poor shorn head looked like a boy's. Her blue eyes were still beautiful, but they did not know what was before them, and Mary herself could never look through them again to tell Laura what she was thinking without saying a word.

'Who can it be at this hour in the morning?' Mary wondered, turning her ear towards the sound of the buggy.

'It's a strange woman alone in a buggy. She's wearing a brown sunbonnet and driving a bay horse,' Laura answered. Pa had said that she must be eyes for Mary.

'Can you think of anything for dinner?' Ma asked. She meant for a company dinner, if the woman stayed till dinner-time.

There was bread and molasses, and potatoes. That was all. This was spring-time, too early for garden vegetables; the cow was dry and the hens had not yet begun to lay their summer's eggs. Only a few small fish were left in Plum Creek. Even the little cottontail rabbits had been hunted until they were scarce.

Pa did not like a country so old and worn out that the hunting was poor. He wanted to go West. For two years he had wanted to go West and take a homestead, but Ma did not want to leave the settled country. And there was no money. Pa had made only two poor wheat crops since the grasshoppers came; he had barely been able to keep out of debt, and now there was the doctor's bill.

Laura answered Ma stoutly, 'What's good enough for us is good enough for anybody!'

The buggy stopped and the strange woman sat in it, looking at Laura and Ma in the doorway. She was a pretty woman, in her neat brown print dress and sunbonnet. Laura felt ashamed of her own bare feet and limp dress and uncombed braids. Then Ma said slowly, 'Why, Docia!'

'I wondered if you'd know me,' the woman said. 'A good deal of water's gone under the bridge since you folks left Wisconsin.'

She was the pretty Aunt Docia who had worn the dress with buttons that looked like blackberries, long ago at the sugaring-off dance at Grandpa's house in the Big Woods of Wisconsin.

She was married now. She had married a widower with two children. Her husband was a contractor, working on the new railroad in the West. Aunt Docia was driving alone in the buggy, all the way from Wisconsin to the railroad camps in Dakota Territory.

She had come by to see if Pa would go with her. Her husband, Uncle Hi, wanted a good man to be storekeeper, book-keeper and timekeeper, and Pa could have the job.

'It pays fifty dollars a month, Charles,' she said.

A kind of tightness smoothed out of Pa's thin cheeks and his blue eyes lighted up. He said slowly, 'Seems like I can draw good pay while I'm looking for that homestead, Caroline.'

Ma still did not want to go West. She looked around the kitchen, at Carrie and at Laura standing there with Grace in her arms.

'Charles, I don't know,' she said. 'It does seem providential, fifty dollars a month. But we're settled here. We've got the farm.'

'Listen to reason, Caroline,' Pa pleaded. 'We can get a hundred and sixty acres out West, just by living on it, and the land's as good as this is, or better. If Uncle Sam's willing to give us a farm in place of the one he drove us off of, in Indian Territory, I say let's take it. The hunting's good in the West, a man can get all the meat he wants.'

Laura wanted so much to go that she could hardly keep from speaking.

'How could we go now?' Ma asked. 'With Mary not strong enough to travel.'

'That's so,' said Pa. 'That's a fact.' Then he asked Aunt Docia, 'The job wouldn't wait?'

'No,' Aunt Docia said. 'No, Charles, Hi is in need of a man, right now. You have to take it or leave it.'

'It's fifty dollars a month, Caroline,' said Pa. 'And a homestead.'

It seemed a long time before Ma said gently, 'Well, Charles, you must do as you think best.'

'I'll take it, Docia!' Pa got up and clapped on his hat. 'Where there's a will, there's a way. I'll go see Nelson.'

Laura was so excited that she could hardly do the housework properly. Aunt Docia helped, and while they worked she told the news from Wisconsin.

Her sister, Aunt Ruby, was married and had two boys and a beautiful little baby girl named Dolly Varden. Uncle George was a lumberjack, logging on the Mississippi. Uncle Henry's folks were all well, and Charley was turning out better than had been expected, considering how Uncle Henry had spared the rod and spoiled that child. Grandpa and Grandma were still living in the old place, their big log house. They could afford a frame house now, but Grandpa declared that good sound oak logs made better walls than thin sawed boards.

Even Black Susan, the cat that Laura and Mary had left behind when they rode away from their little log house in the woods, was still living there. The little log house had changed hands several times, and now it was a corn-crib, but nothing would persuade that cat to live anywhere else. She went right on living in the corn-crib, sleek and plump from rats she caught, and there was hardly a family in all that country that didn't have one of her kittens. They were all good mousers, big-eared and long-tailed like Black Susan.

Dinner was ready in the swept, neat house when Pa came back. He had sold the farm. Nelson was paying two hundred dollars cash for it, and Pa was jubilant. 'That'll square up all we owe, and leave a little something over,' he said. 'How's that, Caroline!'

'I hope it's for the best, Charles,' Ma replied. 'But how –'

'Wait till I tell you! I've got it all figured out,' Pa told her. 'I'll go on with Docia tomorrow morning. You and the girls stay here till Mary gets well and strong, say a couple of months. Nelson's agreed to haul our stuff to the depot, and you'll all come out on the train.'

Laura stared at him. So did Carrie and Ma. Mary said, 'On the train?'

They had never thought of travelling on the train. Laura knew, of course, that people did travel on trains. The trains were often wrecked and the people killed. She was not exactly afraid, but she was excited. Carrie's eyes were big and scared in her peaked little face.

They had seen the train rushing across the prairie, with long, rolling puffs of black smoke streaming back from the engine. They heard its roar and its wild, clear whistle. Horses ran away, if their driver could not hold them when they saw a train coming.

Ma said in her quiet way, 'I am sure we will manage nicely with Laura and Carrie to help me.'

CHAPTER 2

GROWN UP

THERE was a great deal of work to be done, for Pa must leave early next morning. He set the old wagon bows on the wagon and pulled the canvas cover over them; it was almost worn out but it would do for the short trip. Aunt Docia and Carrie helped him pack the wagon, while Laura washed and ironed, and baked hardtack for the journey.

In the midst of it all, Jack stood looking on. Everyone was too busy to notice the old bulldog, till suddenly Laura saw him standing between the house and the wagon. He did not frisk about, cocking his head and laughing, as he used to do. He stood braced on his stiff legs because he was troubled with rheumatism now. His forehead was wrinkled sadly and his stub-tail was limp.

'Good old Jack,' Laura told him, but he did not wag. He looked at her sorrowfully.

'Look, Pa. Look at Jack,' Laura said. She bent and

stroked his smooth head. The fine hairs were grey now. First his nose had been grey and then his jaws, and now even his ears were no longer brown. He leaned his head against her and sighed.

All in one instant, she knew that the old dog was too tired to walk all the way to Dakota Territory under the wagon. He was troubled because he saw the wagon ready to go travelling again, and he was so old and tired.

'Pa!' she cried out. 'Jack can't walk so far! Oh, Pa, we can't leave Jack!'

'He wouldn't hold out to walk it for a fact,' Pa said. 'I'd forgot. I'll move the feed-sack and make a place for him to ride here in the wagon. How'll you like to go riding in the wagon, huh, old fellow?'

Jack wagged one polite wag and turned his head aside. He did not want to go, even in the wagon.

Laura knelt down and hugged him as she used to do when she was a little girl. 'Jack! Jack! We're going West! Don't you want to go West again, Jack?'

Always before he had been eager and joyful when he saw Pa putting the cover on the wagon. He had taken his place under it when they started, and all the long way from Wisconsin to Indian Territory, and back again to Minnesota, he had trotted there in the wagon shade, behind the horses' feet. He had waded through creeks and swum rivers, and every night while Laura slept in the wagon he had guarded it. Every morning, even when his feet were sore from walking, he had been glad with her to see the sun rise and the horses hitched up; he had always been ready for the new day of travelling.

Now he only leaned against Laura and nudged his nose under her hand to ask her to pet him gently. She stroked his grey head and smoothed his ears, and she could feel how very tired he was.

Ever since Mary and Carrie, and then Ma, had been sick

with scarlet fever, Laura had been neglecting Jack. He had always helped her in every trouble before, but he could not help when there was sickness in the house. Perhaps all that time he had been feeling lonely and forgotten.

'I didn't mean it, Jack,' Laura told him. He understood; they had always understood each other. He had taken care of her when she was little, and he had helped her take care of Carrie when Carrie was the baby. Whenever Pa had gone away, Jack had always stayed with Laura to take care of her and the family. He was especially Laura's own dog.

She did not know how to explain to him that he must go now with Pa in the wagon and leave her behind. Perhaps he would not understand that she was coming later on the train.

She could not stay with him long now because there was so much work to be done. But all that afternoon she said to him, 'Good dog, Jack,' whenever she could. She gave him a good supper, and after the dishes were washed and the table set for an early breakfast, she made his bed.

His bed was an old horse blanket, in a corner of the lean-to at the back door. He had slept there ever since they moved into this house, where Laura slept in the attic and he could not climb the attic ladder. For five years he had slept there, and Laura had kept his bed aired and clean and comfortable. But lately she had forgotten it. He had tried to scratch it up and arrange it himself, but the blanket was packed down in hard ridges.

He watched her while she shook it out and made it comfortable. He smiled and wagged, pleased that she was making his bed for him. She made a round nest in it and patted it to show him that it was ready.

He stepped in and turned himself around once. He stopped to rest his stiff legs and slowly turned again. Jack always turned around three times before he lay down to sleep at night. He had done it when he was a young dog in the Big Woods, and he had done it in the grass under the wagon every night. It is a proper thing for dogs to do.

So wearily he turned himself around the third time and curled down with a bump and a sigh. But he held his head up to look at Laura.

She stroked his head where the fine grey hairs were, and she thought of how good he had always been. She had always been safe from wolves or Indians because Jack was there. And how many times he had helped her bring in the cows at night. How happy they had been playing along Plum Creek and in the pool where the fierce old crab had lived, and when she had to go to school he had always been waiting at the ford for her when she came home.

'Good Jack, good dog,' she told him. He turned his head to touch her hand with the tip of his tongue. Then he let his nose sink on to his paws and he sighed and closed his eyes. He wanted to sleep now.

In the morning when Laura came down the ladder into the lamplight, Pa was going out to do the chores. He spoke to Jack, but Jack did not stir.

Only Jack's body, stiff and cold, lay curled there on the blanket.

They buried it on the low slope above the wheatfield, by the path he used to run down so gaily when he was going with Laura to bring in the cows. Pa spaded the earth over the box and made the mound smooth. Grass would grow there after they had all gone away to the West. Jack would never again sniff the morning air and go springing over the short grass with his ears up and his mouth laughing. He would never nudge his nose under Laura's hand again to say he wanted her to pet him. There had been so many times that she might have petted him without being asked, and hadn't.

'Don't cry, Laura,' Pa said. 'He has gone to the Happy Hunting Grounds.'

'Truly, Pa?' Laura managed to ask.

'Good dogs have their reward, Laura,' Pa told her.

Perhaps, in the Happy Hunting Grounds, Jack was running gaily in the wind over some high prairie, as he used to run on the beautiful wild prairies of Indian Territory. Perhaps at last he was catching a jack rabbit. He had tried so often to catch one of those long-eared, long-legged rabbits and never could.

That morning Pa drove away in the rattling old wagon behind Aunt Docia's buggy. Jack was not standing beside Laura to watch Pa go. There was only emptiness to turn to instead of Jack's eyes looking up to say that he was there to take care of her.

Laura knew then that she was not a little girl any more. Now she was alone; she must take care of herself. When you must do that, then you do it and you are grown up. Laura was not very big, but she was almost thirteen years old, and no one was there to depend on. Pa and Jack had gone, and Ma needed help to take care of Mary and the little girls, and somehow to get them all safely to the West on a train.

CHAPTER 3

RIDING IN THE CARS

WHEN the time came, Laura could hardly believe it was real. The weeks and months had been endless, and now suddenly they were gone. Plum Creek, and the house, and all the slopes and fields she knew so well, were gone; she would never see them again. The last crowded days of packing, cleaning, scrubbing, washing and ironing, and the last minute flurry of bathing and dressing were over. Clean and starched and dressed-up, in the morning of a week-day, they sat in a row on the bench in the waiting-room while Ma bought the tickets.

In an hour they would be riding on the railroad cars.

The two satchels stood on the sunny platform outside the waiting-room door. Laura kept an eye on them, and on Grace, as Ma had told her to. Grace sat still in her little starched white lawn dress and bonnet, her feet in small new shoes sticking straight out. At the ticket window, Ma carefully counted money out of her pocket-book.

Travelling on the train cost money. They had not paid anything to travel in the wagon, and this was a beautiful morning to be riding in the wagon along new roads. It was a September day and small clouds were hurrying in the sky. All the girls were in school now; they would see the train go roaring by and know that Laura was riding in it. Trains went faster than horses can run. They went so terribly fast that often they were wrecked. You never knew what might happen to you on a train.

Ma put the tickets inside her mother-of-pearl pocket-book and carefully snapped shut its little steel clasps. She looked so nice in her dark delaine dress with white lace collar and cuffs. Her hat was black straw with a narrow turned-up brim and a white spray of lilies-of-the-valley standing up at one side of the crown. She sat down and took Grace on her lap.

Now there was nothing to do but wait. They had come an hour early to be sure not to miss the train.

Laura smoothed her dress. It was brown calico sprinkled with small red flowers. Her hair hung down her back in long, brown braids, and a red ribbon bow tied their ends together. There was a red ribbon around the crown of her hat too.

Mary's dress was grey calico with sprays of blue flowers. Her wide-brimmed straw hat had a blue ribbon on it. And under the hat, her poor short hair was held back from her face by a blue ribbon tied around her head. Her lovely blue eyes did not see anything. But she said, 'Don't fidget, Carrie, you'll muss your dress.'

Laura craned to look at Carrie, sitting beyond Mary. Carrie was small and thin in pink calico, with pink ribbons on her brown braids and her hat. She flushed miserably because Mary found fault with her, and Laura was going to say, 'You come over by me, Carrie, and fidget all you want to!'

Just then Mary's face lighted up with joy and she said, 'Ma, Laura's fidgeting, too! I can tell she is, without seeing!'

'So she is, Mary,' Ma said, and Mary smiled in satisfaction.

Laura was ashamed that in her thoughts she had been cross with Mary. She did not say anything. She got up and she was passing in front of Ma without saying a word. Ma had to remind her, 'Say "Excuse me," Laura.'

'Excuse me, Ma. Excuse me, Mary,' Laura said politely, and she sat down beside Carrie. Carrie felt safer when she was between Laura and Mary. Carrie was really afraid of going on a train. Of course she would never say that she was frightened, but Laura knew.

'Ma,' Carrie asked timidly, 'Pa will surely meet us, won't he?'

'He is coming to meet us,' Ma said. 'He has to drive in from the camp, and it will take him all day. We are going to wait for him in Tracy.'

'Will he – will he get there before night, Ma?' Carrie asked.

Ma said she hoped so.

You can not tell what may happen when you go travelling on a train. It is not like starting out all together in a wagon. So Laura said bravely, 'Maybe Pa's got our homestead picked out, already. You guess what it's like, Carrie, and then I'll guess.'

They could not talk very well, because all the time they were waiting, and listening for the train. At long, long last, Mary said she thought she heard it. Then Laura heard a faint, far-away hum. Her heart beat so fast that she could hardly listen to Ma.

Ma lifted Grace on her arm, and with her other hand she

took tight hold of Carrie's. She said, 'Laura, you come behind me with Mary. Be careful, now!'

The train was coming, louder. They stood by the satchels on the platform and saw it coming. Laura did not know how they could get the satchels on the train. Ma's hands were full, and Laura had to hold on to Mary. The engine's round front window glared in the sunshine like a huge eye. The smokestack flared upward to a wide top, and black smoke rolled up from it. A sudden streak of white shot up through the smoke, then the whistle screamed a long wild scream. The roaring thing came rushing straight at them all, swelling bigger and bigger, enormous, shaking everything with noise.

Then the worst was over. It had not hit them; it was roaring by them on thick big wheels. Bumps and crashes ran along the freight cars and flat cars and they stopped moving. The train was there, and they had to get into it.

'Laura!' Ma said sharply. 'You and Mary be careful!'

'Yes, Ma, we are,' said Laura. She guided Mary anxiously, one step at a time, across the boards of the platform, behind Ma's skirt. When the skirt stopped, Laura stopped Mary.

They had come to the last car at the end of the train. Steps went up into it, and a strange man in a dark suit and a cap helped Ma climb up them with Grace in her arms. 'Oopsy-daisy!' he said, swinging Carrie up beside Ma. Then he said, 'Them your satchels, ma'am?'

'Yes, please,' Ma said. 'Come, Laura and Mary.'

'Who is he, Ma?' Carrie asked, while Laura helped Mary up the steps. They were crowded in a small place. The man came pushing cheerfully past them, with the satchels, and shouldered open the door of the car.

They followed him between two rows of red velvet seats full of people. The sides of the car were almost solidly made of windows; the car was almost as light as outdoors, and chunks of sunshine slanted across the people and the red velvet.

Ma sat down on one velvet seat and plumped Grace on her lap. She told Carrie to sit beside her. She said, 'Laura, you and Mary sit in this seat ahead of me.'

Laura guided Mary in, and they sat down. The velvet seat was springy. Laura wanted to bounce on it, but she must behave properly. She whispered, 'Mary, the seats are red velvet!'

'I see,' Mary said, stroking the seat with her fingertips. 'What's that in front of us?'

'It's the high back of the seat in front, and it's red velvet too,' Laura told her.

The engine whistled, and they both jumped. The train was getting ready to go. Laura knelt up in the seat to see Ma. Ma looked calm and so pretty in her dark dress with its white lace collar and the sweet tiny white flowers on her hat.

'What is it, Laura?' Ma asked.

Laura asked, 'Who was that man?'

'The brakeman,' Ma said. 'Now sit down and –'

The train jerked, jolting her backward. Laura's chin bumped hard on the seat back, and her hat slid on her head. Again the train jerked, not so badly this time, and then it began to shiver and the depot moved.

'It's going!' Carrie cried out.

The shivering grew faster and louder, the depot slid backward, and under the car the wheels began to beat time. A rub-a-dubdub, a rub-a-dubdub, the wheels went, faster and faster. The lumber-yard and the back of the church and the front of the schoolhouse went by, and that was the last of that town.

The whole car swayed now, in time to the clackety-clacking underneath it, and the black smoke blew by in melting rolls. A telegraph wire swooped up and down beyond the window. It did not really swoop, but it seemed to swoop because it sagged between the poles. It was fastened to green glass knobs that glittered in the sunshine and went dark when the smoke rolled above them. Beyond the wire, grasslands and fields and scattered farmhouses and barns went by.

They went so fast that Laura could not really look at them before they were gone. In one hour that train would go twenty miles – as far as the horses travelled in a whole day.

The door opened, and a tall man came in. He wore a blue coat with brass buttons, and a cap, with

CONDUCTOR

in letters across its front. At every seat he stopped and took tickets. He punched round holes in the tickets with a small machine in his hand. Ma gave him three tickets. Carrie and Grace were so little that they could ride on the train without paying.

The Conductor went on, and Laura said low, 'Oh, Mary! so many shining brass buttons on his coat, and it says CONDUCTOR right across the front of his cap!'

'And he is tall,' Mary said. 'His voice is high up.'

Laura tried to tell her how fast the telegraph poles were going by. She said, 'The wire sags down between them and swoops up again,' and she counted them. 'One – oop! two – oop! three! That's how fast they're going.'

'I can tell it's fast, I can feel it,' Mary said happily.

On that dreadful morning when Mary could not see even sunshine full in her eyes, Pa had said that Laura must see for her. He had said, 'Your two eyes are quick enough, and your tongue, if you will use them for Mary.' And Laura had promised. So she tried to be eyes for Mary, and it was seldom that Mary need ask her, 'See out loud for me, Laura, please.'

'Both sides of the car are windows, close together.' Laura said now. 'Every window is one big sheet of glass, and even the strips of wood between the windows shine like glass, they are so polished.'

'Yes, I see,' and Mary felt over the glass and touched the shining wood with her fingertips.

'The sunshine comes slanting in the south windows, in wide stripes over the red velvet seats and the people. Corners of sunshine fall on the floor, and keep reaching out and going back. Up above the windows the shiny wood curves in from the walls on both sides, and all along the middle of the ceiling there's a higher place. It has little walls of tiny, long, low windows, and you can see blue sky outside them. But outside the big windows, on both sides, the country is going by. The stubble-fields are yellow, and haystacks are by the barns, and little trees are yellow and red in clumps around the houses.

'Now I will see the people,' Laura went on murmuring. 'In front of us is a head with a bald spot on top and side whiskers. He is reading a newspaper. He doesn't look out of the windows at all. Farther ahead are two young men with their hats on. They are holding a big white map and looking at it and talking about it. I guess they're going to look for a homestead too. Their hands are rough and calloused so they're good workers. And farther ahead there's a woman with bright yellow hair and, oh, Mary! the brightest red velvet hat with pink roses –'

Just then someone went by, and Laura looked up. She went on, 'A thin man with bristly eyebrows and long moustaches and an Adam's apple just went by. He can't walk straight the train's going so fast. I wonder what – Oh, Mary! He's turning a little handle on the wall at the end of the car, and water's coming out!

'The water's pouring right into a tin cup. Now he's drinking it. His Adam's apple bobs. He's filling the cup again. He just turns the handle, and the water comes right out. How do you suppose it – Mary! He's set that cup on a little shelf. Now he's coming back.'

After the man had gone by, Laura made up her mind. She asked Ma if she could get a drink of water, and Ma said she might. So she started out.

She could not walk straight. The lurching car made her sway and grab at the seat backs all the way. But she got to the end of the car and looked at the shining handle and spout, and the little shelf under them that held the bright tin cup. She turned the handle just a little, and water came out of the spout. She turned the handle back, and the water stopped. Under the cup there was a little hole, put there to carry away any water that spilled. Laura had never seen anything so fascinating. It was all so neat, and so marvellous, that she wanted to fill the cup again and again. But that would waste the water. So after she drank, she only filled the cup part way, in order not to spill it, and she carried it very carefully to Ma.

Carrie drank, and Grace. They did not want any more, and Ma and Mary were not thirsty. So Laura carried the cup back to its place. All the time the train was rushing on and the country rushing back, and the car swaying, but this time Laura did not touch one seat that she passed. She could walk almost as well as the Conductor. Surely nobody suspected that she had never been on a train before.

Then a boy came walking along the aisle, with a basket on his arm. He stopped and showed it to everyone, and some people took things out of it and gave him money. When he reached Laura, she saw that the basket was full of boxes of candy and of long sticks of white chewing gum. The boy showed them to Ma and said, 'Nice fresh candy, ma'am? Chewing gum?'

Ma shook her head, but the boy opened a box and showed

the coloured candy. Carrie's breath made an eager sound before she knew it.

The boy shook the box a little, not quite spilling the candy out. It was beautiful Christmas candy, red pieces and yellow pieces and some striped red-and-white. The boy said, 'Only ten cents, ma'am, one dime.'

Laura, and Carrie too, knew they could not have that candy. They were only looking at it. Suddenly Ma opened her purse and counted out a nickel and five pennies into the boy's hand. She took the box and gave it to Carrie.

When the boy had gone on, Ma said, excusing herself for spending so much, 'After all, we must celebrate our first train ride.'

Grace was asleep, and Ma said that babies should not eat candy. Ma took only a small piece. Then Carrie came into the seat with Laura and Mary and divided the rest. Each had two pieces. They meant to eat one and save the other for next day, but some time after the first pieces were gone, Laura decided to taste her second one. Then Carrie tasted hers, and finally Mary gave in. They licked those pieces all away, little by little.

They were still licking their fingers when the engine whistled long and loud. Then the car went more slowly, and slowly the backs of shanties went backward outside it. All the people began to gather their things together and put on their hats, and then there was an awful jolting crash, and the train stopped. It was noon, and they had reached Tracy.

'I hope you girls haven't spoiled your dinners with that candy,' Ma said.

'We didn't bring any dinner, Ma,' Carrie reminded her.

Absently Ma replied, 'We're going to eat dinner in the hotel. Come, Laura. You and Mary be careful.'

CHAPTER 4

END OF THE RAILS

Pa was not there at that strange depot. The brakeman set down the satchels on the platform and said, 'If you'll wait a minute, ma'am, I'll take you to the hotel. I'm going there myself.'

'Thank you,' Ma said gratefully.

The brakeman helped unfasten the engine from the train. The fireman, all red and smeared with soot, leaned out of the engine to watch. Then he yanked a bell-rope. The engine went on by itself, puffing and chuffing under the bell's clanging. It went only a little way, then it stopped, and Laura could not believe what she saw. The steel rails under the engine, and the wooden ties between them, turned right around. They turned around in a circle there on the ground till the ends of the rails fitted together again, and the engine was facing backwards.

Laura was so amazed that she could not tell Mary what was happening. The engine went clanging and puffing on another track beside the train. It passed the train and went a little way beyond. The bell clanged, men shouted and made motions with their arms, and the engine came backing, bump! into the rear end of the train. All the cars slam-banged against each other. And there stood the train and the engine, facing back towards the East.

Carrie's mouth was open in amazement. The brakeman laughed at her in a friendly way. 'That's the turn-table,' he told her. 'This is the end of the rails, and we have to turn the engine around so it can take the train back down the line.'

Of course, they would have to do that, but Laura had never thought of it before. She knew now what Pa meant when he spoke of the wonderful times they were living in. There had never been such wonders in the whole history of the world, Pa said. Now, in one morning, they had actually travelled a whole week's journey, and Laura had seen the Iron Horse turn around, to go back the whole way in one afternoon.

For just one little minute she almost wished that Pa was a railroad man. There was nothing so wonderful as railroads, and railroad men were great men, able to drive the big iron engines and the fast, dangerous trains. But of course not even railroad men were bigger or better than Pa, and she did not really want him to be anything but what he was.

There was a long line of freight cars on another track

beyond the depot. Men were unloading the cars into wagons. But they all stopped suddenly and jumped down from the wagons. Some of them yelled, and one big young man began to sing Ma's favourite hymn. Only he did not sings its words. He sang:

> 'There is a boarding house
> Not far away
> Where they have fried ham and eggs
> Three times a day.

> 'Wow! How the boarders yell!
> When they hear that dinner bell!
> Whoop! How those eggs do smell!
> Three times –'

He was singing out these shocking words, and some other men were too, when they saw Ma and stopped. Ma walked on quietly, carrying Grace and holding Carrie's hand. The brakeman was embarrassed. He said quickly, 'We better hurry, ma'am, that's the dinner-bell.'

The hotel was down a short street beyond a few stores and vacant lots. A sign over the sidewalk said, 'Hotel', and under it a man stood swinging a hand-bell. It kept on clanging, and all the men's boots made a beating sound on the dusty street and the board sidewalk.

'Oh, Laura, does it look like it sounds?' Mary asked trembling.

'No,' Laura said. 'It looks all right. It's just a town, and they're just men.'

'It sounds so rough,' Mary said.

'This is the hotel door now,' Laura told her.

The brakeman led the way in, and set down the satchels. The floor needed sweeping. There was brown paper on the walls, and a calendar with a big shiny picture of a pretty girl in a bright yellow wheatfield. All the men went hustling through an open door into a big room beyond, where a long table was covered with a white cloth and set for dinner.

The man who had rung the bell told Ma, 'Yes, ma'am! We've got room for you.' He put the satchels behind the desk and said, 'Maybe you'd like to wash up, ma'am, before you eat?'

In a little room there was a washstand. A large china pitcher stood in a big china bowl, and a roller towel hung on the wall. Ma wet a clean handkerchief and washed Grace's face and hands and her own. Then she emptied the bowl into a pail beside the washstand and filled the bowl with fresh water for Mary and again for Laura. The cold water felt good on their dusty, sooty faces, and in the bowl it turned quite black. There was only a little water for each; then the pitcher was empty. Ma set it neatly in the bowl again when Laura was through. They all wiped on the roller towel. A roller towel was very convenient because its ends were sewed together and it ran around on its roller so that everyone could find a dry place.

Now the time had come to go into the dining-room. Laura dreaded that, and she knew that Ma did, too. It was hard to face so many strangers.

'You all look clean and nice,' Ma said. 'Now remember your manners.' Ma went first, carrying Grace. Carrie followed her, then Laura went, leading Mary. The noisy clatter of eating became hushed when they went into the dining-room, but hardly any of the men looked up. Somehow Ma found empty chairs; then they were all sitting in a row at the long table.

All over the table, thick on the white cloth, stood screens shaped like beehives. Under every screen was a platter of meat or a dish of vegetables. There were plates of bread and of butter, dishes of pickles, pitchers of syrup, and cream pitchers and bowls of sugar. At each place was a large piece of pie on a small plate. The flies crawled and buzzed over the wire screens, but they could not get at the food inside.

Every one was very kind and passed the food. All the dishes kept coming from hand to hand up and down the table to Ma. Nobody talked except to mutter, 'You're welcome, ma'am,' when Ma said, 'Thank you.' A girl brought her a cup of coffee.

Laura cut Mary's meat into small pieces for her and buttered her bread. Mary's sensitive fingers managed her knife and fork perfectly, and did not spill anything.

It was a pity that the excitement took away their appetites. The dinner cost twenty-five cents, and they could eat all they wanted to eat; there was plenty of food. But they ate only a little. In a few minutes all the men finished their pie and left, and the girl who had brought the coffee began to stack up the plates and carry them into the kitchen. She was a big, good-natured girl with a broad face and yellow hair.

'I guess you folks are going out to homestead?' she asked Ma.

'Yes,' Ma said.

'Your man working on the railroad?'

'Yes,' Ma said. 'He's coming here to meet us this afternoon.'

'I thought that's the way it was,' the girl said. 'It's funny your coming out here this time of year, most folks come in the spring. Your big girl's blind, ain't she? That's too bad. Well, the parlour's on the other side of the office; you folks can sit in there if you want to, till your man comes.'

The parlour had a carpet on the floor and flowered paper on the walls. The chairs were cushioned in dark red plush. Ma sank into the rocking-chair with a sigh of relief. 'Grace does get heavy. Sit down, girls, and be quiet.'

Carrie climbed into a big chair near Ma, and Mary and

Laura sat on the sofa. They were all quiet, so that Grace would go to sleep for her afternoon nap.

The centre table had a brass-bottomed lamp on it. Its curved legs ended in glass balls on the carpet. Lace curtains were looped back from the window, and between them Laura could see the prairie, and a road going away across it. Perhaps that was the road that Pa would come on. If it was, they would all go away on that road, and somewhere, far beyond the end of it that Laura could see, some day they would all be living on the new homestead.

Laura would rather not stop anywhere. She would rather go on and on, to the very end of the road, wherever it was.

All that long afternoon they sat quiet in that parlour while Grace slept, and Carrie slept a little, and even Ma dozed. The sun was almost setting when a tiny team and wagon came into sight on the road. It slowly grew larger. Grace was awake now, and they all watched from the window. The wagon grew life-size, and it was Pa's wagon, and Pa was in it.

Because they were in a hotel, they could not run out to meet him. But in a moment he came in saying, 'Hullo! Here's my girls!'

CHAPTER 5

RAILROAD CAMP

EARLY next morning they were all in the wagon going
West. Grace sat between Ma and Pa on the spring seat, and
Carrie and Laura sat with Mary between them on a board
laid across the wagon box.

Travelling on the cars was rich and swift but Laura
preferred the wagon. For this one day's trip, Pa had not
put on the cover. The whole sky was overhead and the
prairie stretched away on all sides with farms scattered over

it. The wagon went slowly, so there was time to see every-thing. And they could all talk comfortably together.

The only noise was the horses' feet clop-clopping and the little creaking sounds of the wagon.

Pa said that Uncle Hi had finished his first contract and was moving to a new camp farther West. He said, 'The men have cleared out already. There's only a couple of teamsters left beside Docia's folks. They'll have the last of the shanties down and be hauling off the lumber in a couple of days.'

'Are we moving on then, too?' Ma asked.

'In a couple of days, yes,' Pa answered. He had not looked for a homestead yet. He would get one farther West.

Laura did not find much to see out loud for Mary. The horses followed the road that went straight across the prairie. Always beside it was the railroad grade of raw earth. To the north the fields and houses were the same as at home, except that they were newer and smaller.

The freshness of the morning wore off. All the time little jolts and jiggles came up from the wagon through the hard board that they were sitting on. It seemed that the sun had never climbed so slowly. Carrie sighed. Her peaked little face was pale. But Laura could do nothing for her. Laura and Carrie must sit on the ends of the board where the jiggling was hardest because Mary must be in the middle.

At last the sun was overhead, and Pa stopped the horses by a little creek. It was good to feel still. The little creek talked to itself, the horses munched their oats in the feed-box at the back of the wagon, and on the warm grass Ma spread a cloth and opened the lunch-box. There was bread and butter and good hardboiled eggs, with pepper and salt in a paper, to dip the bitten eggs into.

Noon ended too soon. Pa led the horses to drink from the creek, while Ma and Laura picked up the eggshells and bits of paper, to leave the place tidy. Pa hitched the horses to the wagon again and sang out, 'All aboard!'

Laura and Carrie wished they could walk for a while. But they did not say so. They knew that Mary could not keep up with the wagon, and they could not let her sit in it alone and blind. They helped her climb up, and sat down beside her on the board.

The afternoon was longer than the morning. Once Laura said, 'I thought we were going West.'

'We are going West, Laura,' Pa said, surprised.

'I thought it would be different,' Laura explained.

'Just you wait till we get out beyond settled country!' said Pa.

Once Carrie sighed, 'I'm tired.' But she straightened up quickly and said, 'Not so very tired.' Carrie did not mean to complain.

One little jolt is nothing at all. They had hardly noticed two miles and a half of little jolts when they rode to town from Plum Creek. But all the little jolts from sunrise to noon, and then all the little jolts from noon to sunset, are tiring.

Dark came, and still the horses plodded on, and the wheels kept turning and the hard board went on jarring. Stars were overhead. The wind was chilly. They would all have been asleep if the jolting board had let them sleep. For a long time nobody said anything. Then Pa said, 'There's the light of the shanty.'

Far ahead there was a little twinkle on the dark land. The stars were larger but their light was cold. The tiny twinkle was warm.

'It's a little yellow spark, Mary,' Laura said. 'It's shining from far away in the dark to tell us to keep on coming, there's a house there, and folks.'

'And supper,' said Mary. 'Aunt Docia's keeping supper hot for us.'

Very slowly the light twinkled larger. It began to shine steady and round. After a long time it was square cornered.

'You can see it's a window now,' Laura told Mary. 'It's in a long, low house. There are two other long, low dark houses in the dark. That's all I can see.'

'That's all of the camp,' Pa said. He told the horses, 'Whoa.'

The horses stopped right then, without another step. The jiggling and jolting stopped. Everything stopped; there was only the still, cold dark. Then lamplight flared out of a doorway and Aunt Docia was saying, 'Come right in, Caroline and girls! Hurry and put up your team, Charles; supper's waiting!'

The chilly dark had settled in Laura's bones. Mary and Carrie moved stiffly too, and they stumbled, yawning. In the long room, the lamp shone on a long table and benches and rough board walls. It was warm there and smelled of supper on the stove. Aunt Docia said, 'Well, Lena and Jean, aren't you going to say anything to your cousins?'

'How do you do?' Lena said. Laura and Mary and Carrie all said, 'How do you do?'

Jean was only a little boy, eleven years old. But Lena was a year older than Laura. Her eyes were black and snappy, her hair was black as black can be, and it curled naturally. The short wisps curled around her forehead, the top of her head was wavy, and the ends of her braids were round curls. Laura liked her.

'Do you like to ride horseback?' she asked Laura. 'We've got two black ponies. We ride them, and I can drive them too. Jean can't because he's too little. Pa won't let him take the buggy. But I can, and tomorrow I'm going for the washing and you can come if you want to, do you?'

'Yes!' Laura said. 'If Ma'll let me.' She was too sleepy to ask how they could go in a buggy for the washing. She was so sleepy that she could hardly stay awake to eat supper.

Uncle Hi was fat and good-natured and easygoing. Aunt Docia talked very fast. Uncle Hi tried to calm her down, but every time he tried, Aunt Docia only talked faster. She was angry because Uncle Hi had worked hard all summer and had nothing to show for it.

'He's worked like a nailer all summer!' she said. 'He's even worked his own teams on the grade, and both of us saving and scrimping and pinching till the job was finished, and now it's finished and the company says we owe them money! They say we're in debt to them for our summer's hard work! And on top of that they want us to take another contract, and Hi takes it! That's what he does! He takes it!'

Uncle Hi tried to calm her down again, and Laura tried to stay awake. All the faces wavered and the voice ravelled out thin; then her neck jerked her head up. When supper was over, she staggered up to help do the dishes, but Aunt Docia told her and Lena to run along to bed.

There was no room in Aunt Docia's beds for Laura and Lena, nor for Jean. He was going to stay in the bunkhouse with the men, and Lena said, 'Come along, Laura! We're going to sleep in the office tent!'

Outdoors was very large and dim and chilly. The bunk-house lay low and dark under the big sky, and the little office tent was ghostly in the starlight. It seemed far away from the lamplit shanty.

The tent was empty. There was only grass underfoot and canvas walls sloping up to a peak overhead. Laura felt lost and lonesome. She would not have minded sleeping in the wagon, but she did not like to sleep on the ground in a strange place, and she wished that Pa and Ma were there.

Lena thought it was great fun to sleep in the tent. She flopped down right away, on a blanket spread on the ground. Laura mumbled sleepily, 'Don't we undress?'

'What for?' Lena said. 'You only have to put on your

clothes again in the morning. Besides, there aren't any covers.'

So Laura lay down on the blanket and was sound asleep. Suddenly she jerked awake with a frightful start. From the huge blackness of the night came again a wild, shrill howl.

It was not an Indian. It was not a wolf. Laura did not know what it was. Her heart stopped beating.

'Aw, you can't scare us!' Lena called out. She said to Laura, 'It's Jean, trying to scare us.'

Jean yelled again, but Lena shouted, 'Run away, little boy! I wasn't brought up in the woods to be scared by an owl!'

'Yah!' Jean called back. Laura began to unstiffen and fell asleep.

CHAPTER 6

THE BLACK PONIES

SUNSHINE, coming through the canvas on to Laura's face, woke her. She opened her eyes just as Lena opened hers, and looking at each other they laughed.

'Hurry up! We're going for the washing!' Lena sang out, jumping up.

They hadn't undressed, so they did not need to dress. They folded the blanket and their bedroom work was done. They went skipping out into the large, breezy morning.

38

The shanties were small under the sunny sky. East and west ran the railroad grade and the road; northward the grasses were tossing tawny seed plumes. Men were tearing down one of the shanties with a pleasant racket of clattering boards. On picket lines in the blowing grasses, the two black ponies, with blowing black manes and tails, were grazing.

'We've got to eat breakfast first,' Lena said. 'Come on, Laura! Hurry!'

Everyone except Aunt Docia was already at the table. Aunt Docia was frying pancakes.

'Get yourselves washed and combed, you lie-abeds! Breakfast's on the table and no thanks to you, lazy miss!' Aunt Docia, laughing, gave Lena a spank as Lena went by. This morning she was as good-natured as Uncle Hi.

Breakfast was jolly. Pa's great laugh rang out like bells. But afterwards what stacks of dishes there were to wash!

Lena said the dishes were nothing to what she had been doing; dishes three times a day for forty-six men, and between times the cooking. She and Aunt Docia had been on their feet from before sunrise till late at night, and still they couldn't keep up with all the work. That's why Aunt Docia had hired the washing out. This was the first time that Laura had ever heard of hiring out the washing. A homesteader's wife did Aunt Docia's washing; she lived three miles away, so they'd have a six-mile drive.

Laura helped Lena carry the harness to the buggy, and lead the willing ponies from their picket lines. She helped put the harness on them, the bits into their mouths, the hames on the collars clasping their warm black necks, and the tailpieces under their tails. Then Lena and Laura backed the ponies in beside the buggy pole, and fastened the stiff leather traces to the whiffletrees. They climbed into the buggy and Lena took the lines.

Pa had never let Laura drive his horses. He said she was not strong enough to hold them if they ran away.

As soon as Lena had the lines, the black ponies started gaily trotting. The buggy wheels turned swiftly, the fresh wind blew. Birds fluttered and sang and flew dipping over the tops of the blowing grasses. Faster and faster went the ponies, faster went the wheels. Laura and Lena laughed with joy.

The trotting ponies touched noses, gave a little squeal and ran.

Up sailed the buggy, almost jerking the seat from under Laura. Her bonnet flapped behind her tugging at its strings around her throat. She clutched on to the seat's edge. The ponies were stretched out low, running with all their might.

'They're running away!' Laura cried out.

'Let 'em run!' Lena shouted, slapping them with the lines. 'They can't run against anything but grass! Hi! Yi! Yi, yi, yee-ee!' she yelled at the ponies.

Their long black manes and tails streamed on the wind, their feet pounded, the buggy sailed. Everything went rushing by too fast to be seen. Lena began to sing:

> 'I know a young man fair to see,
> Take care! Oh, take care!
> And he can very obliging be.
> Beware! Oh, beware!'

Laura had not heard the song before, but she was soon singing the refrain with all her voice.

> 'Take care, dear girl, he's a-fooling you!
> Take care! Oh, take care!
> Trust him not for he won't prove true,
> Beware! Oh, beware!'

'Hi, yi, yi, yi yipee-ee!' they yelled. But the ponies couldn't go faster, they were going as fast as they could.

'I wouldn't marry a farmer (Lena sang)
    He's always in the dirt,
I'd rather marry a railroad man
    Who wears a striped shirt!

'Oh, a railroad man, a railroad man,
    A railroad man for me!
I'm going to marry a railroad man,
    A railroader's bride I'll be!'

'I guess I better breathe them,' she said. She pulled at the lines till she made the ponies trot, and then they slowed to a walk. Everything seemed quiet and slow.

'I wish I could drive,' Laura said. 'I always wanted to, but Pa won't let me.'

'You can drive aways,' Lena offered generously.

Just then the ponies touched noses again, squealed and ran.

'You can drive on the way home!' Lena promised. Singing and whooping, they went racing on across the prairie. Every time Lena slowed the ponies to get their breath, they got it and ran again. In no time at all, they reached the homesteader's claim shanty.

It was a tiny room, boarded up-and-down, and its roof sloped all one way, so that it looked like half of a little house. It was not as big as the wheat stacks beyond it, where men were threshing wheat with a noisy, chaff-puffing machine. The homesteader's wife came out to the buggy, lugging the basket of washing. Her face and arms and her bare feet were as brown as leather from the sun. Her hair straggled uncombed and her limp dress was faded and not clean.

'You must excuse the way I look,' she said. 'My girl was married yesterday, and here come the threshers this morning, and this wash to do. I been hustling since before sun-up, and here the day's work hardly started and my girl not here any more to help me.'

'Do you mean Lizzie got married?' Lena asked.

'Yes, Lizzie got married yesterday,' Lizzie's mother said proudly. 'Her Pa says thirteen's pretty young, but she's got her a good man and I say it's better to settle down young. I was married young myself.'

Laura looked at Lena, and Lena looked at her. On the way back to camp they did not say anything for some time. Then both spoke at once.

'She was only a little older than I am,' said Laura, and Lena said, 'I'm a year older than she was.'

They looked at each other again, an almost scared look. Then Lena tossed her curly black head. 'She's a silly! Now she can't ever have any more good times.'

Laura said soberly, 'No, she can't play any more now.'

Even the ponies trotted gravely. After a while Lena said she supposed that Lizzie did not have to work any harder than before. 'Anyway, now she's doing her own work in her own house, and she'll have babies.'

'Well,' Laura said, 'I'd like my own house and I like babies, and I wouldn't mind the work, but I don't want to be so responsible. I'd rather let Ma be responsible for a long time yet.'

'And besides, I don't want to settle down,' Lena said. 'I'm not ever going to get married, or if I do, I'm going to marry a railroader and keep on moving West as long as I live.'

'May I drive now?' Laura asked. She wanted to forget about growing up.

Lena gave her the lines. 'All you have to do is hold the lines,' Lena said. 'The ponies know the way back.' At that instant, the ponies touched noses and squealed.

'Hold on to them, Laura! Hold on to them!' Lena screeched.

Laura braced her feet and hung on to the lines with all her might. She could feel that the ponies didn't mean any harm. They were running because they wanted to run in the windy weather; they were going to do what they wanted to do. Laura hung on to them and yelled, 'Yi, yi, yi, yip-ee!'

She had forgotten the basket of clothes, and so had Lena. All the way back to camp across the prairie they went whooping and singing, the ponies went running, trotting, and running again. When they stopped by the shanties to unhitch and picket the ponies, they found all the top layers of the clean washing on the buggy floor under the seats.

Guiltily they piled and smoothed them and lugged the heavy basket into the shanty where Aunt Docia and Ma were dishing up the dinner.

'You girls look as if butter wouldn't melt in your mouths,' said Aunt Docia. 'What have you been up to?'

'Why, we just drove out and brought back the washing,' said Lena.

That afternoon was even more exciting than the morning. As soon as the dishes were washed, Lena and Laura ran out again to the ponies. Jean had gone on one of them. He was riding away at a run across the prairie.

'Not fair!' Lena yelled. The other pony was galloping in a circle, held by its picket rope. Lena grabbed its mane, unsnapped the rope, and sailed right up from the ground on to the back of the running pony.

Laura stood watching Lena and Jean race in circles, yelling like Indians. They rode crouching, their hair streaming back, their hands clutched in the flying black manes and their brown legs clasping the ponies' sides. The ponies curved and swerved, chasing each other on the prairie like birds in the sky. Laura would never have tired of watching them.

The ponies came galloping and stopped near her, and Lena and Jean slid off.

'Come on, Laura,' Lena said generously. 'You can ride Jean's pony.'

'Who says she can?' Jean demanded. 'You let her ride your own pony.'

'You better behave or I'll tell how you tried to scare us last night,' said Lena.

Laura took hold of the pony's mane. But the pony was much larger than she was, its back was high, and the pony was strong. Laura said, 'I don't know if I can. I never did ride horseback.'

'I'll put you on,' said Lena. She held her pony by the forelock with one hand, and bending down she held her other hand for Laura to step on to.

Jean's pony seemed larger every minute. It was big and strong enough to kill Laura if it wanted to, and so high that to fall off it would break her bones. She was so scared to ride it that she had to try.

She stepped on to Lena's hand, she scrambled up the warm, slippery, moving mass of pony, while Lena boosted. Then she got one leg over the pony's back and everything began moving rapidly. Dimly she heard Lena saying, 'Hang on to his mane.'

She was holding on to the pony's mane. She was hanging on to deep handfuls of it with all her might, and her elbows and her knees were holding on to the pony, but she was jolting so that she couldn't think. The ground was so far beneath that she didn't dare look. Every instant she was falling, but before she really fell she was falling the other way, and the jolting rattled her teeth. Far off she heard Lena yell, 'Hang on, Laura!'

Then everything smoothed into the smoothest rippling motion. This motion went through the pony and through Laura and kept them sailing over waves in rushing air. Laura's screwed-up eyes opened, and below her she saw the grasses flowing back. She saw the pony's black mane blow-

44

ing, and her hands clenched tight in it. She and the pony were going too fast but they were going like music and nothing could happen to her until the music stopped.

Lena's pony came pounding along beside her. Laura wanted to ask how to stop safely but she could not speak. She saw the shanties far ahead, and knew that somehow the ponies had turned back towards the camp. Then the jolting began again. Then it stopped, and there she sat on the pony's back.

'Didn't I tell you it's fun?' Lena asked.

'What makes it jolt so?' Laura asked.

'That's trotting. You don't want to trot, you want to make your pony gallop. Just yell at it, like I did. Come on, let's go a long ways this time, you want to?'

'Yes,' said Laura.

'All right, hang on. Now, yell!'

That was a wonderful afternoon. Twice Laura fell off; once the pony's head hit her nose and made it bleed, but she never let go of the mane. Her hair came unbraided and her throat grew hoarse from laughing and screeching, and her legs were scratched from running through the sharp grass and trying to leap on to her pony while it was running. She almost could, but not quite, and this made the pony mad. Lena and Jean always started the ponies to running and then swung up. They raced each other from the ground, trying which could sooner mount and reach a certain mark.

They did not hear Aunt Docia calling them to supper. Pa came out and shouted, 'Supper!' When they went in, Ma looked at Laura in shocked amazement and said mildly, 'Really, Docia, I don't know when Laura's looked so like a wild Indian.'

'She and Lena are a pair,' said Aunt Docia. 'Well, Lena hasn't had an afternoon to do as she liked since we came out here, and she won't have another till the summer's over.'

CHAPTER 7

THE WEST BEGINS

EARLY next morning they were all in the wagon again. It had not been unloaded so everything was ready to go.

Nothing was left of the camp but Aunt Docia's shanty. Over the worn-out grass and the dead spots where shanties had been, surveyors were measuring and driving stakes for a new town that would be built.

'We'll be along as soon as Hi gets his business settled,' Aunt Docia said.

'I'll see you at Silver Lake!' Lena called to Laura, while Pa chirruped to the horses and the wheels began to turn.

The sun shone brightly on the uncovered wagon, but the wind was cool and riding was pleasant. Here and there, men were working in their fields, and now and then a team and wagon passed.

Soon the road curved downward through rolling land and Pa said, 'The Big Sioux River's ahead.'

Laura began to see out loud for Mary. 'The road's going down a low bank to the river, but there aren't any trees. There's just the big sky and grassy land, and the little, low creek. It's a big river sometimes, but now it's dried up till it's no bigger than Plum Creek. It trickles along from pool to pool, by dry gravel stretches and cracked dry mud flats. Now the horses are stopping to drink.'

'Drink hearty,' Pa said to the horses. 'There's no more water for thirty miles.'

Beyond the low river the grassy land was low curve behind curve and the road looked like a short hook.

'The road pushes against the grassy land and breaks off short. And that's the end of it,' said Laura.

'It can't be,' Mary objected. 'The road goes all the way to Silver Lake.'

'I know it does,' Laura answered.

'Well, then I don't think you ought to say things like that,' Mary told her gently. 'We should always be careful to say exactly what we mean.'

'I was saying what I meant,' Laura protested. But she could not explain. There were so many ways of seeing things and so many ways of saying them.

Beyond the Big Sioux there were no more fields, no houses, no people in sight. There really was no road, only a dim wagon trail, and no railroad grade. Here and there Laura glimpsed a little wooden stake, almost hidden in the grasses. Pa said they were surveyors' stakes for the railroad grade that was not started yet.

Laura said to Mary, 'This prairie is like an enormous

meadow, stretching far away in every direction, to the very edge of the world.'

The endless waves of flowery grasses under the cloudless sky gave her a queer feeling. She could not say how she felt. All of them in the wagon, and the wagon and team, and even Pa, seemed small.

All morning Pa drove steadily along the dim wagon track, and nothing changed. The farther they went into the West, the smaller they seemed, and the less they seemed to be going anywhere. The wind blew the grass always with the same endless rippling, the horses' feet and the wheels going over the grass made always the same sound. The jiggling of the board seat was always the same jiggling. Laura thought they might go on for ever, yet always be in this same changeless place, that would not even know they were there.

Only the sun moved. Without ever seeming to, the sun moved steadily upward in the sky. When it was overhead, they stopped to feed the horses and to eat a picnic lunch on the clean grass.

It was good to rest on the ground after riding all the morning. Laura thought of the many times they had eaten under the sky, while they were travelling all the way from Wisconsin to Indian Territory and back again to Minnesota. Now they were in Dakota Territory going farther West. But this was different from all the other times, not only because there was no cover on the wagon and no beds in it, but some other reason. Laura couldn't say how, but this prairie was different.

'Pa,' she asked, 'when you find the homestead, will it be like the one we had in Indian Territory?'

Pa thought before he answered. 'No,' he said finally. 'This is different country. I can't tell you how, exactly, but this prairie is different. It feels different.'

'That's likely enough,' Ma said sensibly. 'We're west of

Minnesota, and north of Indian Territory, so naturally the flowers and grasses are not the same.'

But that was not what Pa and Laura meant. There was really almost no difference in the flowers and grasses. But there was something else here that was not anywhere else. It was an enormous stillness that made you feel still. And when you were still, you could feel great stillness coming closer.

All the little sounds of the blowing grasses and of the horses munching and whooshing in their feed-box at the back of the wagon, and even the sounds of eating and talking could not touch the enormous silence of this prairie.

Pa talked about his new job. He would be the company storekeeper, and the timekeeper at Silver Lake camp. He would run the store and he would keep straight in his books the charge account of every man on the job, and know exactly how much money was due each man for his work, after his board bill and his account at the store had been subtracted. And when the paymaster brought the money each payday, Pa would pay every man. That was all he had to do, and for that he would be paid fifty dollars every month.

'And best of all, Caroline, we're among the very first out here!' said Pa. 'We've got the pick of the land for our homestead. By George, our luck's turned at last! First chance at new land, and fifty dollars a month for a whole summer to boot!'

'It is wonderful, Charles,' said M a.

But all their talking did not mean anything to the enormous silence of that prairie.

All that afternoon they went on, mile after mile, never seeing a house or any sign of people, never seeing anything but grass and sky. The trail they followed was marked only by bent and broken grasses.

Laura saw old Indian trails and buffalo paths worn deep

in the ground and now grassed over. She saw strange large depressions, straight-sided and flat-bottomed, that had been buffalo wallows, where now the grass was growing. Laura had never seen a buffalo, and Pa said it was not likely that she would ever see one. Only a little while before the vast herds of thousands of buffaloes had grazed over this country. They had been the Indians' cattle, and white men had slaughtered them all.

On every side now the prairie stretched away empty to far, clear skyline. The wind never stopped blowing, waving the tall prairie grasses that had turned brown in the sun. And all the afternoon, while Pa kept driving onward, he was merrily whistling or singing. The song he sang oftenest was:

> 'Oh, come to this country,
> And don't you feel alarm,
> For Uncle Sam is rich enough
> To give us all a farm!'

Even baby Grace joined in the chorus, though she did not bother to follow the tune.

> 'Oh, come away! Come away!
> Come away, I say!
> Oh, come away! Come away!
> Come right away!
> Oh, come to this country
> And have no fear of harm
> Our Uncle Sam is rich enough
> To give us all a farm!'

The sun was lowering in the West when a rider appeared on the prairie behind the wagon. He came following behind not very fast, but coming a little nearer mile after mile while the sun was slowly sinking.

'How much farther is it to Silver Lake, Charles?' Ma asked.

'About ten miles,' said Pa.

'There isn't anybody living nearer, is there?'

'No,' said Pa.

Ma did not say anything more. Neither did anyone else. They kept glancing back at that rider behind them, and each time they looked, he was a little nearer. He was surely following them and not meaning to overtake them until the sun sank. The sun was so low that every hollow between the low prairie swells was filled with shadow.

Each time that Pa glanced back, his hand made a little motion, slapping the horses with the lines to hurry them. But no team could pull a loaded wagon as fast as a man could ride.

The man was so near now that Laura could see two pistols in leather holsters on his hips. His hat was pulled low over his eyes, and a red bandana was tied loosely around his neck.

Pa had brought his gun West, but it was not in the wagon now. Laura wondered where it was, but she did not ask Pa.

She looked back again and saw another rider coming on a white horse. He wore a red shirt. He and the white horse were far behind and small, but they came fast, galloping. They overtook the first rider, and the two came on together.

Ma said in a low voice, 'There's two of them now, Charles.'

Mary asked frightened, 'What is it? Laura, what's the matter?'

Pa looked back quickly, and then he was comfortable. 'Everything's all right now,' he said. 'That's Big Jerry.'

'Who's Big Jerry?' Ma asked.

'He's a half-breed, French and Indian,' Pa answered carelessly. 'A gambler, and some say a horse thief, but a darned good fellow. Big Jerry won't let anybody waylay us.'

Ma looked at him astonished. Her mouth opened and then it shut; she did not say anything.

The riders came up beside the wagon. Pa lifted his hand and said, 'Hullo, Jerry!'

'Hullo, Ingalls!' Big Jerry answered. The other man gave them all a snarling look and went galloping on ahead, but Big Jerry rode along by the wagon.

He looked like an Indian. He was tall and big but not one bit fat, and his thin face was brown. His shirt was flaming red. His straight black hair swung against his flat, high-boned cheek as he rode, for he wore no hat. And his snow-white horse wore no saddle nor bridle. The horse was free, he could go where he wanted to go, and he wanted to go with Big Jerry wherever Big Jerry wanted to ride. The horse and the man moved together as if they were one animal.

They were beside the wagon only a moment. Then away they went in the smoothest, prettiest run, down into a little hollow and up and away, straight into the blazing round sun on the far edge of the West. The flaming red shirt and the white horse vanished in the blazing golden light.

Laura let out her breath. 'Oh, Mary! The snow-white horse and the tall, brown man, with such a black head and a bright red shirt! The brown prairie all around – and they rode right into the sun as it was going down. They'll go on in the sun around the world.'

Mary thought a moment. Then she said, 'Laura, you know he couldn't ride into the sun. He's just riding along on the ground like anybody.'

But Laura did not feel that she had told a lie. What she had said was true too. Somehow that moment when the beautiful, free pony and the wild man rode into the sun would last for ever.

Ma still feared that the other man might be lying in wait to rob them, but Pa told her, 'Don't worry! Big Jerry's gone ahead to find him and stay with him till we get into camp. Jerry'll see that nobody molests us.'

Ma looked back to see that her girls were all right, and she held Grace snugly on her lap. She did not say anything because nothing she could say would make any difference. But Laura knew that Ma had never wanted to leave Plum Creek and did not like to be here now; she did not like travelling in that lonely country with night coming on and such men riding the prairie.

The wild calls of birds came down from the fading sky. More and more dark lines streaked the pale-blue air overhead – straight lines of wild ducks, and long flying wedges of wild geese. The leaders called to their flocks behind them, and each bird answered in turn. The whole sky twanged, 'Honk? Honk! Honk! Quanck? Quanck. Quanck.'

'They're flying low,' said Pa. 'Settling down for the night on the lakes.'

There were lakes ahead. A thin silvery line at the very edge of the sky was Silver Lake, and little glimmers south of it were the Twin Lakes, Henry and Thompson. A wee dark blob between them was the Lone Tree. Pa said it was a big cottonwood, the only tree to be seen between the Big Sioux River and the Jim; it grew on a little rise of ground no wider than a road, between the Twin Lakes, and it grew big because its roots could reach water.

'We'll get some seeds from it to plant on our homestead,' Pa said. 'You can't see Spirit Lake from here, it's nine miles north-west of Silver Lake. You see, Caroline, what fine hunting country this is. Plenty of water and good feeding ground for wild fowl.'

'Yes, Charles, I see,' said Ma.

The sun sank. A ball of pulsing, liquid light, it sank in clouds of crimson and silver. Cold purple shadows rose in the east, crept slowly across the prairie, then rose in heights on heights of darkness from which the stars swung low and bright.

The wind, which all day long had blown strongly, dropped low with the sun and went whispering among the tall grasses. The earth seemed to lie breathing softly under the summer night.

Pa drove on and on beneath the low stars. The horses' feet went softly thump-thumping on the grassy ground. Far, far ahead a few tiny lights pricked through the dark. They were the lights of Silver Lake camp.

'Don't need to see the trail for these next eight miles,' Pa told Ma. 'All a man's got to do is keep driving towards the lights. There's nothing between us and camp but smooth prairie and air.'

Laura was tired and chilly. The lights were far away. They might be stars after all. The whole night was a glittering of stars. Close overhead and down on all sides great stars glittered in patterns on the dark. The tall grass rustled against the turning wagon wheels; it kept on rustling, rustling against the wheels that kept on turning.

Suddenly Laura's eyes jerked open. There was an open doorway and light streaming out. And in the dazzle of lamplight Uncle Henry was coming, laughing. So this must be Uncle Henry's house in the Big Woods when Laura was little, for that was where Uncle Henry was.

'Henry!' Ma exclaimed.

'It's a surprise, Caroline!' Pa sang out. 'I thought I wouldn't tell you Henry's out here.'

'I declare, it takes my breath, I am so surprised,' said Ma.

And then a big man was laughing up at them, and he was Cousin Charley. He was the big boy who had bothered Uncle Henry and Pa in the oatfield, and been stung by thousands of yellow jackets. 'Hello, Half-pint! Hello, Mary! And here's baby Carrie, a big girl now. Not the baby any longer, uh?' Cousin Charley helped them down from the wagon, while Uncle Henry took Grace and Pa helped Ma over the wheel, and here came Cousin Louisa, bustling and talking and herding them all into the shanty.

Cousin Louisa and Charley were both grown up now. They were keeping the boarding shanty, cooking for the men who were working on the grade. But the men had eaten supper long ago, and now they were all sleeping in the bunkhouses. Cousin Louisa talked about all this, while she dished up the supper she had been keeping hot on the stove.

After supper Uncle Henry lighted a lantern and led the way to a shanty that the men had built for Pa.

'It's all new lumber, Caroline, fresh and clean as a whistle,' Uncle Henry said, holding up the lantern so they could see the new board walls and the bunks built up against them. There was a bunk on one side for Ma and Pa, and on the other side two narrow bunks, one above the other, for Mary and Laura and Carrie and Grace. The beds were already spread in the bunks; Cousin Louisa had seen to that.

In no time at all, Laura and Mary were cuddled on the rustling fresh hay-mattress with the sheet and quilts drawn up to their noses, and Pa blew out the lantern.

CHAPTER 8

SILVER LAKE

THE sun had not yet risen next morning when Laura let down the pail into the shallow well by Silver Lake. Beyond the lake's eastern shore the pale sky was bordered with bands of crimson and gold. Their brightness stretched around the south shore and shone on the high bank that stood up from the water in the east and the north.

Night was still shadowy in the north-west, but Silver Lake lay like a sheet of silver in its setting of tall wild grasses.

Ducks quacked among the thick grasses to the south-west, where the Big Slough began. Screaming gulls flew over the lake, beating against the dawn wind. A wild goose rose from the water with a ringing call, and one after another the birds of his flock answered him as they rose and

56

followed. The great triangle of wild geese flew with a beating of strong wings into the glory of the sunrise.

Shafts of golden light shot higher and higher in the eastern sky, until their brightness touched the water and was reflected there.

Then the sun, a golden ball, rolled over the eastern edge of the world.

Laura breathed a long breath. Then hurriedly she pulled up the pail of water, and carrying it she hurried back towards the shanty. The new shanty stood alone by the lake shore, south of the cluster of shanties that was the graders' camp. It shone yellow in the sunshine; a little house almost lost in the grasses, and its little roof sloped all one way, as if it were only half a roof.

'We have been waiting for the water, Laura,' Ma said, when Laura went in.

'Oh, but Ma! the sunrise! You should have seen the sunrise!' Laura exclaimed. 'I just had to watch it.'

She began quickly to help Ma get breakfast, and while she hurried she told how the sun came up beyond Silver Lake, flooding the sky with wonderful colours while the flocks of wild geese flew dark against them, how thousands of wild ducks almost covered the water, and gulls flew screaming against the wind above it.

'I heard them,' Mary said. 'Such a clamouring of wild birds, it was like bedlam. And now I see it all. You make pictures when you talk, Laura.'

Ma smiled at Laura too, but she only said, 'Well, girls, we have a busy day before us,' and she laid out their work.

Everything must be unpacked and the shanty made tidy before noon. Cousin Louisa's beds must be aired and returned, and Ma's ticking mattresses stuffed with fresh clean hay. Meanwhile, from the company store Ma brought yards of bright-figured calico for curtains. She made a curtain and they hung it across the shanty, shutting the bunks in behind it. Then she made another curtain and hung it between the bunks; so there were two bedrooms, one for her and Pa, the other for the girls. The shanty was so small that the curtains touched the bunks, but when the bunks were made up with Ma's mattresses and featherbeds and patchwork quilts, it all looked fresh and bright and snug.

Then in front of the curtain was the room to live in. It was very small, with the cookstove at the end by the door. Ma and Laura placed the drop-leaf table against the side wall, before the open front door. Mary's rocking-chair and Ma's they put on the other side of the room. The floor was bare ground, with humps of obstinate grass roots in it, but they swept it clean. The wind blew softly in from the open doorway, and the railroad shanty was very pleasant and homelike.

'This is another kind of little house with only half a roof and no window,' said Ma. 'But it's a tight roof, and we don't need a window, so much air and light come through the doorway.'

When Pa came to dinner, he was pleased to see everything so nicely settled and arranged. He tweaked Carrie's ear and swung Grace up in his hands; he could not toss her, under that low roof.

'But where's the china shepherdess, Caroline?' he asked.

'I haven't unpacked the shepherdess, Charles,' said Ma. 'We aren't living here, we're only staying till you get our homestead.'

Pa laughed. 'I've got plenty of time to pick the right one too! Look at all this great prairie with nobody on it but the railroad graders and they'll go away before winter comes. We can just about take our pick of the land.'

'After dinner,' Laura said, 'Mary and I are going to take a walk and look at the camp and the lake and everything.'

She took the water pail and ran out bareheaded to get fresh water from the well for dinner.

The wind was blowing steady and strong. Not a cloud was in the huge sky, and far and wide on the immense land there was nothing but shimmering light passing over the grasses. And down wind came the sound of many men's voices, singing.

The teams were coming into camp. In a long, dark, snake-like line they came over the prairie, horses plodding side by side in their harness, and men marching, bare-headed and bare-armed, brown-skinned in their striped blue-and-white shirts and grey shirts and plain blue shirts, and all of them were singing the same song.

They were like a little army coming across the vast land under the enormous empty sky, and the song was their banner.

Laura stood in the strong wind, looking and listening, till the last of the column came into the crowd that gathered and spread around the camp's low shanties, and the song blurred into the sound of all their hearty voices. Then she remembered the water pail in her hand. She filled it from the well as quickly as she could, and ran back; slopping water on her bare legs in her hurry.

'I just had – to watch the – teams coming into camp,' she panted. 'So many of them, Pa! And all the men were singing!'

'Now, Flutterbudget, catch your breath!' Pa laughed at her. 'Fifty teams and seventy-five or eighty men are only a small camp. You ought to see Stebbins' camp west of here; two hundred men and teams according.'

'Charles,' Ma said.

Usually everyone knew what Ma meant when she said in her gentle way, 'Charles.' But this time Laura and Carrie and Pa all looked at her wondering. Ma shook her head just the least bit at Pa.

Then Pa looked straight at Laura and said, 'You girls keep away from the camp. When you go walking, don't go near where the men are working, and you be sure you're back here before they come in for the night. There's all kinds of rough men working on the grade and using rough language, and the less you see and hear of them the better. Now remember, Laura. And you too, Carrie.' Pa's face was very serious.

'Yes, Pa,' Laura promised, and Carrie almost whispered, 'Yes, Pa.' Carrie's eyes were large and frightened. She did not want to hear rough language, whatever rough language might be. Laura would have liked to hear some, just once, but of course she must obey Pa.

So that afternoon when they set out for their walk they went away from the shanties. They set out along the lake shore towards the Big Slough.

The lake lay at their left shimmering in the sunshine. Little silvery waves rose and fell and lapped upon the shore as the wind ruffled the blue water. The shore was low, but firm and dry, with little grasses growing to the water's edge. Across the glittering lake, Laura could see the east bank and the south bank, rising up as tall as she was. A little slough came into the lake from the north-east, and Big Slough went on towards the south-west in a long curve of tall wild grasses.

Laura and Mary and Carrie walked slowly along on the green shore by the rippling silver-blue water, towards the wild Big Slough. The grasses were warm and soft to their feet. The wind blew their flapping skirts tight against their bare legs and ruffled Laura's hair. Mary's sunbonnet and Carrie's were tied firmly under their chins, but Laura swung hers by its strings. Millions of rustling grass-blades made one murmuring sound, and thousands of wild ducks and geese and herons and cranes and pelicans were talking sharply and brassily in the wind.

All those birds were feeding among the grasses of the sloughs. They rose on flapping wings and settled again, crying news to each other and talking among themselves among the grasses, and eating busily of grass roots and tender water plants and little fishes.

The lake shore went lower and lower towards Big Slough, until really there was no shore. The lake melted into the slough, making small ponds surrounded by the harsh, rank slough grass that stood five and six feet tall. Little ponds glimmered between the grasses and on the water the wild birds were thick.

As Laura and Carrie pushed into the slough grasses, suddenly harsh wings ripped upward and round eyes glittered; the whole air exploded in a noise of squawking, quacking, quonking. Flattening their webbed feet under their tails, ducks and geese sped over the grass-tops and curved down to the next pond.

Laura and Carrie stood still. The coarse-stemmed slough grass rose above their heads and made a rough sound in the wind. Their bare feet sank slowly into ooze.

'Oo, the ground is all soft,' Mary said, turning back quickly. She did not like mud on her feet.

'Go back, Carrie!' Laura cried. 'You'll mire down! The lake is in here among the grasses!'

The soft, cool mud sucked around her ankles as she stood, and before her the little ponds glimmered among the tall grasses. She wanted to go on and on, into the slough among the wild birds, but she could not leave Mary and Carrie. So she turned back with them to the hard, higher prairie where waist-high grasses were nodding and bending in the wind, and the short, curly buffalo grass grew in patches.

Along the edge of the slough they picked flaming red tiger lilies, and on higher ground they gathered long branching stems of purple buffalo bean pods. Grasshoppers flew up like spray before their feet in the grasses. All kinds of little birds fluttered and flew and twittered balancing in the wind on the tall, bending grass stems, and prairie hens scuttled everywhere.

'Oh, what a wild, beautiful prairie!' Mary sighed with happiness. 'Laura, have you got your sunbonnet on?'

Guiltily Laura pulled up her sunbonnet from where it hung by its strings down her neck. 'Yes, Mary,' she said.

Mary laughed. 'You just now put it on. I heard you!'

It was late afternoon when they turned back. The little shanty, with its roof slanting all one way, stood all by itself and small at the edge of Silver Lake. Tiny in the doorway, Ma shaded her eyes with her hand to look for them, and they waved to her.

They could see the whole camp, scattered along the lake shore north of the shanty. First was the store where Pa was working with the big feed store behind it. Then the stable for the work teams. The stable was built into a swell of the prairie, and its roof was thatched with slough grass. Beyond it was the long, low bunkhouse where the men slept, and still farther away was Cousin Louisa's long boarding-house shanty, with supper smoke already rising from its stovepipe.

Then for the first time Laura saw a house, a real house, standing all by itself on the lake's northern shore.

'I wonder what that house can be and who lives there,' she said. 'It isn't a homestead because there's no stable and no land ploughed.'

She had told Mary all that she saw, and Mary said, 'What a pretty place it is with the clean, new shanties and the grass and the water. There's no use wondering about that house; we can ask Pa about it. Here comes another flock of wild ducks.'

Flock after flock of ducks and long lines of wild geese were coming down from the sky and settling to stay all night on the lake. And the men were making a racket of voices as they came from their work. In the shanty's doorway again, Ma waited till they reached her, windblown and full of the fresh air and sunshine, bringing her their armfuls of tiger lilies and purple bean pods.

Then Carrie put the big bouquet in a pitcher of water while Laura set the table for supper. Mary sat in her rocking-chair with Grace in her lap and told her about the ducks quacking in the Big Slough and the great flocks of wild geese going to sleep on the lake.

CHAPTER 9

HORSE THIEVES

ONE night at supper Pa spoke hardly at all. He only answered questions. At last Ma asked, 'Aren't you feeling
well, Charles?'

'I'm all right, Caroline,' Pa answered.

'Then what is the matter?' Ma demanded.

'Nothing,' Pa said. 'Nothing to worry you about. Well,
the fact is, the boys have got word to look out for horse
thieves tonight.'

'That's Hi's affair,' Ma said. 'I hope you'll let him tend
to it.'

'Don't worry, Caroline,' Pa said.

Laura and Carrie looked at each other and then at Ma.
After a moment Ma said gently, 'I wish you'd out with it,
Charles.'

'Big Jerry's been in camp,' Pa said. 'He's been here a

week, and now he's gone. The boys say he's in with the gang of horse thieves. They say every time Big Jerry visits a camp the best horses are stolen after he leaves. They think he stays just long enough to pick out the best teams and find out what stalls they're in, and then he comes back with his gang in the night and gets away with them in the dark.'

'I always heard you can't trust a half-breed,' Ma said. Ma did not like Indians; she did not like even half-Indians.

'We'd all have been scalped down on the Verdigris River, if it hadn't been for a full-blood,' said Pa.

'We wouldn't have been in any danger of scalping if it hadn't been for those howling savages,' said Ma, 'with fresh skunk skins around their middles.' And she made a sound that came from remembering how those skunk skins smelled.

'I don't think Jerry steals horses,' Pa said. But Laura thought he said it as if he hoped that saying it would make it so. 'The real trouble is, he comes to camp after payday and wins all the boys' money playing poker. That's why some of them would be glad to shoot him.'

'I wonder Hi allows it,' said Ma. 'If there's anything as bad as drink, it's gambling.'

'They don't have to gamble if they don't want to, Caroline,' Pa said. 'If Jerry wins their money, it's their own fault. There never was a kinder-hearted man than Big Jerry. He'd give the shirt off his back. Look how he takes care of Old Johnny.'

'That's so,' Ma admitted. Old Johnny was the water boss. He was a little, wizened, bent-backed old Irishman. He had worked on railroads all his life, and now he was too old to work. So the company had given him the job of carrying water to the men.

Every morning and again after dinner, little old Johnny came to the well to fill his two large, wooden water pails.

When they were full he set his wooden yoke across his shoulders and, stooping, he hooked into the pails the two hooks that hung from short chains at each end of the yoke. Then with a grunt and groan, he straightened up. The chains lifted the heavy pails from the ground and Johnny steadied them with his hands while he bore their weight on his shoulders. He trotted under the weight with short, stiff steps.

There was a tin dipper in each water pail. When he got to the men working on the grade, Johnny would trot along the line of work, so that any thirsty man could help himself to a drink of water without stopping work.

Johnny was so old that he was little, stooped and shrunken. His face was a mass of wrinkles, but his blue eyes twinkled cheerily and he always trotted as quickly as he could so that no thirsty man need wait for a drink.

One morning before breakfast, Big Jerry had come to the door and told Ma that Old Johnny had been sick all night.

'He's so little and old, ma'am,' Big Jerry said. 'The meals at the boarding shanty don't agree with him. Would you give him a cup of hot tea and a bit of breakfast?'

Ma put several of her hot, light biscuits on a plate and beside them she put a fried mashed-potato cake and a slice of crisply fried salt pork. Then she filled a little tin pail with hot tea and gave it all to big Jerry.

After breakfast Pa went to the bunkhouse to see Old Johnny, and later he told Ma that Jerry had taken care of the poor old man all night. Johnny said that Jerry had even spread his own blanket over him to keep him warm and gone without any covering himself in the cold.

'He couldn't take better care of his own father than he did of Old Johnny,' Pa said. 'For that matter, Caroline, I don't know but what we're beholden to him ourselves.'

They all remembered how Big Jerry had come out of

the prairie on his white horse when the strange man was following them and the sun was setting.

'Well,' Pa said, getting up slowly, 'I've got to go sell the boys the ammunition for their guns. I hope Jerry don't come back to camp tonight. If he just rode up to see how Old Johnny is, rode up to the stable to put his horse in, they'd shoot him.'

'Oh, no, Charles! Surely they wouldn't do that!' Ma exclaimed.

Pa pulled on his hat. 'The one that's doing most of the talking's already killed one man,' he said. 'He got off easy on a plea of self-defence, but he's served a term in State's prison. And Big Jerry cleaned him out, last payday. He hasn't got the nerve to face Big Jerry, but he'll ambush him if he gets the chance.'

Pa went to the store, and Ma soberly began to clear the table. While Laura washed the dishes, she thought of Big Jerry and his white horse. She had seen them many times, galloping over the brown prairie. Big Jerry always wore a bright red shirt, he was always bareheaded, and his white horse never wore a strap.

The night was dark when Pa came from the store. He said that half a dozen men with loaded guns were lying in wait around the stable.

It was bed-time. There was not a light in the camp. The dark shanties, low against the land, could hardly be seen; only if you knew where to look, you could see them darker in the dark. There was a little starshine on Silver Lake, and all around it stretched the black prairie, flat under the velvet-dark sky sparkling with stars. The wind whispered cold in the dark, and the grass rustled as if it were afraid. Laura looked and listened, and hurried shivering into the shanty again.

Behind the curtain Grace was sleeping and Ma was helping Mary and Carrie to bed. Pa had hung up his hat and sat down on the bench, but he was not taking off his boots. He looked up when Laura came in, and then he got up and put on his coat. He buttoned it all the way up and turned up its collar so that his grey shirt did not show. Laura did not say a word. Pa put on his hat.

'Don't sit up for me, Caroline,' he said cheerfully.

Ma came from behind the curtain, but Pa was gone. She went to the doorway and looked out. Pa had disappeared in the darkness. After a minute Ma turned around and said, 'Bed-time, Laura.'

'Please, Ma, let me stay up too,' Laura begged.

'I believe I won't go to bed,' said Ma. 'Not for a while, anyway. I'm not sleepy. It's no use to go to bed when you're not sleepy.'

'I'm not sleepy, Ma,' Laura said.

Ma turned down the lamp and blew it out. She sat down in the hickory rocker that Pa had made for her in Indian territory. Laura went softly on her bare feet across the ground and sat close beside Ma.

They sat in the dark, listening. Laura could hear a thin, faint humming in her ears; it seemed to be the sound of her listening. She could hear Ma's breathing and the slow breathing of Grace, asleep, and the faster breathing of Mary and Carrie lying awake behind the curtain. The curtain made a faint sound, moving a little in the air from the open doorway. Outside the doorway there was an oblong of sky and stars above the faraway edge of dark land.

Out there the wind sighed, the grass rustled, and there was the tiny, ceaseless sound of little waves lapping on the lake shore.

A sharp cry in the dark jerked all through Laura; she almost screamed. It was only the call of a wild goose, lost from its flock. Wild geese answered it from the slough, and a quacking of sleepy ducks rose.

'Ma, let me go out and find Pa,' Laura whispered.

'Be quiet,' Ma answered. 'You couldn't find Pa. And he doesn't want you to. Be quiet and let Pa take care of himself.'

'I want to do something. I'd rather do something,' Laura said.

'So would I,' said Ma. In the dark her hand began softly to stroke Laura's head. 'The sun and the wind are drying your hair, Laura,' Ma said. 'You must brush it more. You must brush your hair a hundred strokes every night before you go to bed.'

'Yes, Ma,' Laura whispered.

'I had lovely long hair when your Pa and I were married,' Ma said. 'I could sit on the braids.'

She did not say any more. She went on stroking Laura's rough hair while they listened for the sound of shooting.

There was one shining large star by the black edge of the doorway. As time went on, it moved. Slowly, it moved from east to west, and more slowly still the smaller stars wheeled about it.

Suddenly Laura and Ma heard footsteps, and in an instant the stars were blotted out. Pa was in the doorway. Laura jumped up, but Ma only went limp in the chair.

'Sitting up, Caroline?' Pa said. 'Pshaw, you didn't need to do that. Everything's all right.'

'How do you know that, Pa?' Laura asked. 'How do you know Big Jerry —'

'Never mind, Flutterbudget!' Pa stopped her cheerfully. 'Big Jerry's all right. He won't be coming into camp to-night. I wouldn't be surprised though, if he rode in this morning on his white horse. Now go to bed. Let's get what sleep we can before sunrise.' Then Pa's great laugh rang out like bells. 'There'll be a sleepy bunch of men working on the grade today!'

While Laura was undressing behind the curtain and Pa was taking off his boots on the other side of it, she heard him say in a low voice to Ma, 'The best of it is, Caroline, there'll never be a horse stolen from Silver Lake camp.'

Sure enough, early that morning Laura saw Big Jerry riding by the shanty on his white horse. He hailed Pa at the store and Pa waved to him; then Big Jerry and the white horse galloped on and away towards where the men were working.

There never was a horse stolen from Silver Lake camp.

CHAPTER 10

THE WONDERFUL AFTERNOON

EARLY every morning while Laura washed the breakfast dishes, she could look through the open door and see the men leaving the boarding shanty and going to the thatched stable for their horses. Then there was a rattling of harness and a confusion of talking and shouts, and the men and teams went out to the job leaving quietness behind them.

All the days went by, one like another. On Mondays Laura helped Ma do the washing and bring in the clean-scented clothes that dried quickly in the wind and sun-shine. On Tuesdays she sprinkled them and helped Ma iron them. On Wednesdays she did her task of mending and sew-ing though she did not like to. Mary was learning to sew without seeing; her sensitive fingers could hem nicely, and she could sew quilt-patches if the colours were matched for her.

At noon the camp was noisy again with all the teams and the men coming in to dinner. Then Pa came from the store, and they all ate in the little shanty with the wind blowing against it and the wide prairie outside the door. Softly coloured in all shades from dark brown to russet and tan, the prairie rolled in gentle swells to the far edge of the sky. The winds were blowing colder at night, more and more wild birds were flying southward, and Pa said that winter would not be long in coming. But Laura did not think about winter.

She wanted to know where the men were working and how they made a railroad grade. Every morning they went out, and at noon and at night they came back, but all that she saw of working was a smudge of dust that came up from the tawny prairie in the west. She wanted to see the men building the railroad.

Aunt Docia moved into the camp one day, and she brought two cows. She said, 'I brought our milk on the hoof, Charles. It's the only way to get any, out here where there aren't any farmers.'

One of the cows was for Pa. She was a pretty, bright-red cow named Ellen. Pa untied her from the back of Aunt Docia's wagon, and handed the halter rope to Laura. 'Here, Laura,' he said. 'You're old enough to take care of her. Take her out where the grass is good, and be sure to drive down the picket pin good and firm.'

Laura and Lena picketed the cows not far apart in good grass. Every morning and every evening they met to take care of the cows. They led them to drink from the lake, and moved the picket pins to fresh grass, and then they did the milking, and while they milked they sang.

Lena knew many new songs and Laura learned them quickly. Together, while the milk streamed into the bright tin pails, they sang:

> 'A life on the ocean wave,
> A home on the rolling deep,
> The pollywogs wag their tails
> And the tears roll down their cheeks.'

Sometimes Lena sang softly, and so did Laura.

> 'Oh, I wouldn't marry a farmer,
> He's always in the dirt,
> I'd rather marry a railroad man
> Who wears a striped shirt.'

But Laura liked the waltz songs best. She loved the Broom song, though they had to sing 'broom' so many times to make the tune swing.

> 'Buy a broo-oom, buy a broom, broom!
> Buy a broom, broom, buy a broom, broom!
> Will you buy of this wandering Bavarian a broom?
> To brush off the insects
> That come to annoy you,
> You'll find it quite useful
> By night and by day.'

The cows stood quiet, chewing their cuds, as though they were listening to the singing until the milking was done.

Then with the pails of warm, sweet-smelling milk, Laura and Lena walked back towards the shanties. In the mornings the men were coming out of the bunkhouse, washing in the basins on the bench by the door and combing their hair. And the sun was rising over Silver Lake.

In the evenings the sky flamed with red and purple and gold, the sun had set, and the teams and men were coming in, dark along the dusty road they had worn on the prairie, and singing. Then quickly Lena hurried to Aunt Docia's shanty, and Laura to Ma's, because they must strain the milk before the cream began to rise, and help get supper.

Lena had so much work to do, helping Aunt Docia and Cousin Louisa, that she had no time to play. And Laura, though she did not work so hard, was busy enough. So they hardly ever met except at milking time.

'If Pa hadn't put our black ponies to work on the grade,' Lena said one evening, 'you know what I'd do?'

'No, what?' Laura asked.

'Well, if I could get away, and if we had the ponies to ride, we'd go see the men working,' said Lena. 'Don't you want to?'

'Yes, I want to,' Laura said. She did not have to decide whether or not she would disobey Pa, because they couldn't do it anyway.

Suddenly one day at dinner Pa set down his teacup, wiped his moustache, and said: 'You ask too many questions, Flutterbudget. Put on your bonnet and come up to the store along about two o'clock. I'll take you out and let you see for yourself.'

'Oh, Pa!' Laura cried out.

'There, Laura, don't get so excited,' Ma said quietly.

Laura knew she should not shout. She kept her voice low. 'Pa, can Lena go too?'

'We will decide about that later,' said Ma.

After Pa had gone back to the store, Ma talked seriously to Laura. She said that she wanted her girls to know how to behave, to speak nicely in low voices and have gentle manners and always be ladies. They had always lived in wild, rough places, except for a little while on Plum Creek, and now they were in a rough railroad camp, and it would be some time before this country was civilized. Until then, Ma thought it best that they keep themselves to themselves.

She wanted Laura to stay away from the camp, and not get acquainted with any of the rough men there. It would be all right for her to go quietly with Pa to see the work this once, but she must be well-behaved and ladylike, and remember that a lady never did anything that could attract attention.

'Yes, Ma,' Laura said.

'And Laura, I do not want you to take Lena,' said Ma. 'Lena is a good, capable girl, but she is boisterous, and Docia has not curbed her as much as she might. If you must go where those rough men are working in the dirt, then go quietly with your Pa and come back quietly, and say no more about it.'

'Yes, Ma,' Laura said. 'But –'

'But what, Laura?' Ma asked.

'Nothing,' said Laura.

'I don't know why you want to go anyway,' Mary wondered. 'It's much nicer here in the shanty, or taking a little walk by the lake.'

'I just want to. I want to see them building a railroad,' Laura said.

She tied on her sunbonnet when she set out and resolved to keep it tied on. Pa was alone in the store. He put on his broad-brimmed hat and padlocked the door, and they went out on the prairie together. At that time of day when there were no shadows the prairie looked level, but it was not. In a few minutes its swells hid the shanties, and on the grassy land there was nothing to be seen but the dusty track of the road and the railroad grade beside it. Against the sky ahead rose up the smudge of dust, blowing away on the wind.

Pa held on to his hat and Laura bent her head in the flapping sunbonnet, and they trudged along together for some time. Then Pa stopped and said, 'There you are, Half-pint.'

They were standing on a little rise of the land. Before them the railroad grade ended bluntly. In front of it, men with teams and ploughs were ploughing onward towards the West, breaking a wide strip of the prairie sod.

'Do they do it with ploughs?' Laura said. It seemed strange to her to think that men with ploughs went ahead into this country that had never been ploughed to build a railroad.

'And scrapers,' said Pa. 'Now watch, Laura.'

Between the ploughing and the blunt end of the grade, teams and men were going slowly around in a circle, over the end of the grade and back to cross the ploughed strip. The teams were pulling wide, deep shovels. These were the scrapers.

Instead of one long shovel handle, each scraper had two short handles. And a strong half-hoop of steel curved from one side of the scraper to the other. The team was hitched to this curve of steel.

When a man and his team came to the ploughed land, another man took hold of the scraper handles and held them just high enough to thrust the round shovel point into the loose earth of the ploughed ground while the team went on and earth filled the scraper. Then he let go of the handles, the full scraper sat level on the ground, and the horses pulled it on around the circle, up the side of the grade.

On the grade's blunt end the man who drove the team caught hold of the scraper's handles and tipped the whole scraper over in a somersault inside the curving steel that the horses were hitched to. All the earth was left right there, while the team drew the empty scraper down the grade and on around the circle to the ploughed land again.

There the other man caught hold of the handles and held them just high enough to thrust the round shovel point into the loose earth until the scraper was filled again. And on around the circle it came sliding behind the team, up the steep slope of the grade, and somersaulting over again.

Team after team came around the circle, scraper after scraper tipped over. The teams never stopped coming, the scrapers never stopped filling and tipping.

As the loose soil was scraped from the ploughed land, the curve widened out so that the scrapers passed over freshly ploughed ground ahead, while the plough teams came back and ploughed again the ground that had been scraped.

'It all goes like clockwork,' said Pa. 'See, no one stands still, no one hurries.

'When one scraper is filled another is on the spot to take its place, and the scraper holder is there to grab the handles and fill it. The scrapers never have to wait for the ploughs, and the ploughs go just so far ahead before they come back to plough again the ground that has been scraped. They are doing great work. Fred is a good boss.'

Fred stood on the dump watching the teams and scrapers circling, and the ploughs coming around inside the circle and moving out ahead of it again. He watched the dumping of the scrapers and the earth rolling down, and with a nod or a word he told each driver when to dump his scraper, so that the grade would be even, and straight, and level.

For every six teams, one man did nothing but stand and watch. If a team slowed, he spoke to the driver and he drove faster. If a team went too fast, he spoke to that driver and that driver held his horses back. The teams must be spaced evenly, while they kept on going steadily around the circle, over the ploughed land and to the grade and over it and back to the ploughed land again.

Thirty teams and thirty scrapers, and all the four-horse teams and the ploughs, and all the drivers and the scraper holders, all were going round and round, all in their places and all moving in time, there on the open prairie, just like the works of a clock as Pa had said, and on the prow of the new railroad grade in the dust, Fred, the boss, kept it all going.

Laura would never have tired of watching that. But farther west there was more to see. Pa said, 'Come along, Half-pint, and see how they make a cut and a fill.'

Laura walked with Pa along the wagon track, where the crushed dead grasses were like broken hay in the dust where wagon wheels had passed. Farther to the west, beyond a little rise of the prairie, more men were building another piece of the railroad grade.

In the little dip beyond the rise they were making a fill, and farther on they were making a cut through higher ground.

'You see, Laura,' Pa said, 'where the ground is low, they make the grade higher, and where the ground is high they cut through it to make the grade level. A railroad road-bed has to be as level as it can be for the trains to run on.'

'Why, Pa?' Laura asked. 'Why can't the trains just run over the prairie swells?' There were no real hills, and it seemed a waste of hard work to cut through all the little rises and fill in all the little hollows, just to make the road-bed level.

'No, it saves work, later on,' Pa said. 'You ought to be able to see that, Laura, without being told.'

Laura could see that a level road would save work for horses, but a locomotive was an iron horse that never got tired.

'Yes, but it burns coal,' said Pa. 'Coal has to be mined, and that's work. An engine burns less coal running on a level than it does going up and down grades. So you see it takes more work and costs more money now to make a level grade, but later on there'll be a saving in work and money, so they'll be used for building something else.'

'What, Pa? What else?' Laura asked.

'More railroads,' said Pa. 'I wouldn't wonder if you'll

live to see a time, Laura, when pretty nearly everybody'll ride on railroads and there'll hardly be a covered wagon left.'

Laura could not imagine a country with so many railroads, nor one so rich that nearly everybody could ride on trains, but she did not really try to imagine it because now they had come to high ground where they could see the men working at the cut and the fill.

Right across the prairie swell where the trains would run, the teams with ploughs and the teams with scrapers were cutting a wide ditch. Back and forth went the big teams pulling the ploughs, and round and round went the teams hauling the scrapers, all steadily moving in time with each other.

But here the scrapers did not go in a circle; they went in a long, narrow loop, into the cut and out again at one end, and at the other end they went over the dump.

The dump was a deep ditch at the end of the cut, and crossways to it. Heavy timbers shored up the sides of this ditch and made a flat platform over the top of it. There was a hole in the middle of this platform, and earth had been graded high on each side of the ditch, to make a road level with the platform.

Out of the cut came the teams steadily walking one behind another pulling the loaded scrapers. They went up the grade to the top of the dump and they went across the platform. They passed over the hole, one horse walking on each side of it, while into the hole the driver dumped the scraper-load of soil. Going steadily on, down the steep grade and around, they went back into the cut to fill the scraper again.

All the time, a circle of wagons was moving through the dump, under the hole in the platform. Every time a scraper dumped its load, a wagon was under the hole to catch the soil. Each wagon waited till five scraper-loads had poured down into it, then it moved on and the wagon behind it moved under the hole and waited.

The circle of wagons came out of the dump and curved back to climb up over the end of the high railroad grade that was coming towards the cut. Every wagon, as it passed over the grade, dumped its load and made the grade that much longer. The wagons had no wagon-boxes; they were only platforms of heavy planks. To dump the soil the teamster turned those planks over, one at a time. Then he drove onward, down over the end of the fill and back in the endless circle, through the dump to be loaded again.

Dust blew from the ploughs and the scrapers, and from the dump and the end of the hill. A great cloud of dust rose all the time, up over the sweating men and the sweating horses. The men's faces and arms were black with sunburn and dust, their blue and grey shirts were streaked with sweat and dust, and the horses' manes and tails and hair were full of dust and their flanks were caked with muddy sweat.

They all went on, steadily and evenly, circling into the cut and out while the ploughs went back and forth, and circling under the dump and back over the end to the fill and under the dump again. The cut grew deeper and the fill grew longer while the men and teams kept on weaving their circles together, never stopping.

'They never miss once,' Laura marvelled. 'Every time a scraper dumps, there's a wagon underneath to catch the earth.'

'That's the boss's job,' Pa said. 'He makes them keep time just like they were playing a tune. Watch the boss, and you'll see how it's done. It's pretty work.'

On the rise above the cut and on the end of the fill and along the circles, the bosses stood. They watched the men and the teams and kept them moving in time. Here they slowed one team a little, there they hurried another. No one stopped and waited. No one was late at his place.

Laura heard the boss call out from the top of the cut. 'Boys! Move along a little faster!'

'You see,' Pa said, 'it's nearing quitting time, and they'd all slowed down a little. They can't put that over on a good boss.'

The whole afternoon had gone while Pa and Laura watched those circles moving, making the railroad grade. It was time to go back to the store and the shanty. Laura took one last, long look, and then she had to go.

On the way, Pa showed her the figures painted on the little grade-stakes that were driven into the ground in a straight line where the railroad grade would be. The surveyors had driven those stakes. The figures told the graders how high to build the grade on low ground, and how deep to make the cuts on high ground. The surveyors had measured it all and figured the grade exactly, before anyone else had come there.

First, someone had thought of a railroad. Then the surveyors had come out to that empty country, and they had marked and measured a railroad that was not there at all; it was only a railroad that someone had thought of. Then the ploughmen came to tear up the prairie grass, and the scraper-men to dig up the soil, and the teamsters with their wagons to haul it. And all of them said they were working on the railroad, but still the railroad wasn't there. Nothing was there yet but cuts through the prairie swells, pieces of the railroad grade that were really only narrow, short ridges of earth, all pointing westward across the enormous grassy land.

'When the grade's finished,' Pa said, 'the shovel-men will come along with bank shovels, and they'll smooth the sides of the grade by hand, and level it on top.'

'And then they'll lay the rails,' Laura said.

'Don't jump ahead so fast, Flutterbudget.' Pa laughed at her. 'The railroad ties have got to be shipped out here and laid before it's time for the rails. Rome wasn't built in a day, and neither's a railroad, nor anything else worth having.'

The sun was so low now that each prairie swell began to have its shadow lying eastward, and out of the large, pale sky the flocks of ducks and the long wedges of geese were sliding down to Silver Lake to rest for the night. The clean wind was blowing now with no dust in it, and Laura let her sunbonnet slip down her back so that she could feel the wind on her face and see the whole great prairie.

There was no railroad there now, but someday the long steel tracks would lie level on the fills and through the cuts, and trains would come roaring, steaming and smoking with speed. The tracks and the trains were not there now, but Laura could see them almost as if they were there.

Suddenly she asked, 'Pa, was that what made the very first railroad?'

'What are you talking about?' Pa asked.

'Are there railroads because people think of them first when they aren't there?'

Pa thought a minute. 'That's right,' he said. 'Yes, that's what makes things happen, people think of them first. If enough people think of a thing and work hard enough at it, I guess it's pretty nearly bound to happen, wind and weather permitting.'

'What's that house, Pa?' Laura asked.

'What house?' Pa asked.

'That house, that real house.' Laura pointed. All this time she had been meaning to ask Pa about that house standing by itself on the north shore of the lake, and she had always forgotten.

'That's the surveyors' house,' Pa said.

'Are they there now?' Laura asked.

'They come and go,' said Pa. They had almost reached the store, and he went on. 'Run on along home now, Flutterbudget. I've got work to do on the books. Now you know how a railroad grade's made, be sure to tell Mary all about it.'

'Oh, I will, Pa!' Laura promised. 'I'll see it out loud for her, every bit.'

She did her best, but Mary only said, 'I really don't know, Laura, why you'd rather watch those rough men working in the dirt than stay here in the nice clean shanty. I've finished another quilt patch while you've been idling.'

But Laura was still seeing the movement of men and horses in such perfect time that she could almost sing the tune to which they moved.

CHAPTER 11

PAYDAY

Two weeks had gone by and now Pa worked every evening after supper in his little office at the back of the store. He was making out the time-checks.

From the time-book he counted up the days each man had worked, and figured how much he had earned. Then Pa figured up how much the man owed the store; to that he added the man's board-bill at the cook-shanty. He subtracted that amount from the man's wages, and made out his time-check.

On payday Pa would give each man his time-check and the money due him.

Always before, Laura had helped Pa with his work. When she was very little, in the Big Woods, she had helped him make the bullets for his gun; in Indian Territory she had helped finish the house, and on Plum Creek she had helped with the chores and the haying. But she could not help him now, for Pa said that the railroad company would not want anyone but him to work in the office.

Still she always knew what he was doing, for the store was in plain sight from the shanty's doorway and she saw everyone who came and went.

One morning she saw a fast team come dashing up to the store's door, and a man in fine clothes got quickly out of the buggy and hurried into the store. Two more men waited in the buggy, watching the door and looking around them on every side as if they were afraid.

In a little while the first man came out and got into the buggy. After another look all around, they drove away quickly.

Laura ran out of the shanty towards the store. She was sure that something had happened there. Her heart was beating wildly, and it gave a great flop when she saw Pa, safe and sound, come out of the store.

'Where are you going, Laura?' Ma had called after her, and now Laura answered, 'Nowhere, Ma.'

Pa came into the shanty and swung the door shut behind him. He took a heavy canvas bag out of his pocket.

'I want you to take care of this, Caroline,' he said. 'It's the men's pay. Anybody that tried to steal it would come to the office.'

'I'll take care of it, Charles,' Ma said. She wrapped the bag in a clean cloth and worked it deep into her open sack of flour. 'Nobody'll ever think of looking there for it.'

'Did that man bring it, Pa?' Laura asked.

'Yes. That was the paymaster,' said Pa.

'Those men with him were afraid,' Laura said.

'Oh, I wouldn't say that. They were only guarding the paymaster to keep him from being robbed,' Pa said. 'He's carrying a good many thousand dollars in cash to pay all the men in the camps, and somebody might try to get it. But those men had guns enough on them and in the buggy. They had no need to be afraid.'

As Pa went back to the store, Laura saw the handle of his revolver showing from his hip pocket. She knew he was not afraid, and she looked at his rifle over the door and his shotgun standing in the corner. Ma could use those guns. There was no fear that robbers could get that money.

That night Laura woke up often, and often she heard Pa stirring, too, in the bunk on the other side of the curtain. The night seemed darker and full of strange sounds, because that money was in the flour-sack. But no one would think of looking for it there, and no one did.

Early in the morning, Pa took it to the store. This was payday. After breakfast all the men gathered around the store, and one by one they went inside. One by one they came out again, and stood in little groups, talking. They would not work that day; it was payday.

At supper Pa said he must go back to the office again. 'Some of the men don't seem to understand why they got only two weeks' pay,' he said.

'Why don't they get paid for the whole month?' Laura asked him.

'Well, you see, Laura, it takes time to make out all those time-checks and send them in, and then the paymaster has to bring out the money. I'm paying the men their wages now up to the fifteenth, and in another two weeks I'll pay them up to now. Some of them can't get it through their thick heads that they've got to wait two weeks for their pay. They want to be paid right up to yesterday.'

'Don't fret about it, Charles,' said Ma. 'You can't expect them to understand how business is handled.'

'And they don't blame you, do they, Pa?' said Mary.

'That's the worst of it, Mary. I don't know,' Pa answered. 'Anyway I've got some bookwork to do at the office.'

The supper dishes were soon washed, and Ma sat rocking Grace to sleep, with Carrie snuggled beside her. Laura sat beside Mary in the doorway, watching the light fade from the waters of the lake. She was seeing it out loud for Mary.

'The last light is shining pale in the middle of the smooth lake. All around it the water is dusky, where the ducks sleep, and the land is black beyond. The stars are beginning to twinkle in the grey sky. Pa has lighted his lamp. It shines out yellow from the back of the black store. Ma!' she cried out. 'There's a big crowd of men – look.'

The men were crowding around the store. They did not say anything, and there was not even any sound of their feet on the grass. Only the dark mass of men was growing larger very fast.

Ma rose quickly and laid Grace on the bed. Then she came and looked out over Laura's head and Mary's. She spoke softly. 'Come inside, girls.'

When they obeyed her she shut the door, all but a crack. She stood looking out through the crack.

Mary sat in the chair with Carrie, but Laura peeped under Ma's arm. The crowd was close around the store. Two men went up the step and pounded on the door.

The crowd was quiet. The whole dusky twilight was quiet for a moment.

Then the men pounded again on the door and one called, 'Open the door, Ingalls!'

The door opened, and there in the lamplight stood Pa. He shut the door behind him, and the two men who had knocked stepped backward into the crowd. Pa stood on the step with his hands in his pockets.

'Well, boys, what is it?' he asked quietly.

A voice came from the crowd. 'We want our pay.'

Other voices shouted. 'Our full pay!' 'Come across with that two weeks' pay you kept back!' 'We're going to get our pay!'

'You'll have it two weeks from now, just as soon as I can get your time-checks made out,' said Pa.

The voices shouted again. 'We want it now!' 'Quit stalling!' 'We're going to have it now!'

'I can't pay you now, boys,' Pa said. 'I won't have the money to pay you till the paymaster comes again.'

'Open up the store!' somebody answered. Then the whole crowd yelled. 'That's it! That's good enough – Open the store! Open up that store!'

'No, boys. I won't do that,' Pa said coolly. 'Come in tomorrow morning, and I'll let each man have all the goods he wants, on his account.'

'Open up that store or we'll open it for you!' came a shout. A growl rumbled from the crowd. The whole mass of men moved in towards Pa as if that growl moved them.

Laura ducked under Ma's arm, but Ma's hand clenched on her shoulder and pulled her back.

'Oh, let me go! They'll hurt Pa! Let me go, they'll hurt Pa!' Laura screamed in a whisper.

'Be still!' Ma told her in a voice Laura had never heard before.

'Stand back, boys. Don't crowd too close,' said Pa. Laura heard his cold voice and stood trembling.

Then she heard another voice behind the crowd. It was deep and strong, not loud, but plainly heard. 'What's up, boys?'

In the dark Laura could not see the red shirt, but only Big Jerry was so tall. He stood head and shoulders above the shadowy figures of the crowd. Beyond them in the dusk was a pale blur that would be the white horse. A confusion of voices answered Big Jerry, then he laughed. His laugh was big and booming.

'You fools!' Big Jerry laughed. 'What's the fuss about? You want the goods out of the store? Well, tomorrow we'll take what we want of them. They'll still be here. Nobody'll stop us when we get started.'

Laura was hearing rough language. Big Jerry was using it. What he said was all mixed with swear words and with other words she had never heard. She hardly heard them now, because she felt all broken up; she felt as if everything was smashed like a dropped plate when Big Jerry took sides against Pa.

The crowd was all around Big Jerry now. He was calling some of the men by their names and talking to them about drinking and playing cards. Some of the crowd went with him towards the bunkhouse, then the rest of it broke into smaller pieces and scattered away in the dark.

Ma shut the door. 'Bed-time, girls,' she said.

Laura went trembling to bed as Ma told her to do. Pa did not come. Now and then she heard an outbreak of loud, rough voices from the camp, and sometimes singing. She knew she would not sleep till Pa came.

Then her eyes opened suddenly. It was morning.

Beyond Silver Lake the sky was burning gold and one line of red cloud lay across it; the lake was rosy, and wild birds flew up clamouring. The camp was noisy too. All around the boarding shanty the men were gathered in a milling crowd, talking excitedly.

Ma and Laura stood outdoors at the corner of the shanty watching. They heard a shout and saw Big Jerry jump on to his white horse.

'Come on, boys!' he shouted. 'All aboard for the fun!'

The white horse reared and whirled and reared again. Big Jerry gave a wild whoop, the white horse broke into a run, and away they went over the prairie towards the west. All the men rushed to the stable and in a minute man after man was on his horse and following Big Jerry. The whole crowd went streaming away on the horses and was gone.

A great, cool quietness came over the camp and over Laura and Ma. 'Well!' Ma said.

They saw Pa walking from the store towards the boarding shanty. Fred, the foreman, came out of it and met him. They talked a minute. Then Fred went to the stable, got on his horse, and galloped away to the west.

Pa was chuckling. Ma said she did not know what there was to laugh about.

'That Big Jerry!' Pa's laugh rang out. 'By gum, if he didn't lead 'em all away to do their devilment somewhere else!'

'Where?' Ma asked sharply.

Pa was sober then. 'There's a riot at Stebbins' camp. Everybody's flocking there from all the camps. You're right, Caroline, it's no laughing matter.'

All day the camp was quiet. Laura and Mary did not go for their walk. There was no telling what might be happening at Stebbins' camp, nor when that dangerous crowd would come back. Ma's eyes were anxious all day, her lips were tight, and now and then she sighed without knowing it.

After dark the men came. But they rode into camp more quietly than they had left. They ate supper in the boarding shanty and then they went to bed in the bunkhouse.

Laura and Mary were still awake when Pa came late from the store. They lay quiet in their bunk and heard Pa and Ma talking beyond the lamp-lit curtain.

'Nothing to worry about now, Caroline,' Pa said. 'They're tired out and everything's quiet.' He yawned, and sat down to take off his boots.

'What did they do, Charles? Was anybody hurt?' Ma asked.

'They strung up the paymaster,' said Pa. 'And one man was hurt bad. They put him in a lumber wagon and started back East with him to find a doctor. Don't get so upset, Caroline. We better thank our stars we got off so easy. It's all over.'

'I don't get upset till it is over,' Ma said. Her voice was shaking.

'Come here,' said Pa. Laura knew that now Ma was sitting on Pa's knee. 'There, I know you don't,' he said to her. 'Never mind, Caroline. The grading's pretty near done, these camps'll be closing down and gone before long, and next summer we'll be settled on the homestead.'

'When are you going to pick it out?' said Ma.

'Quick as the camps close. I don't have a minute away from the store till then,' said Pa. 'You know that.'

'Yes, I know, Charles. What did they do about the men that – killed the paymaster?'

'They didn't kill him,' Pa said. 'It was this way. You see, it's the same at Stebbins' camp as here; the office is a lean-to at the back of the store. It has one door into the store and that's all. The paymaster stayed in the office with the money and kept the door locked. He paid the men through a little opening beside the door.

'Stebbins has got over three hundred and fifty men drawing pay there, and they wanted their pay up to now, like the men here wanted it. When they got paid only to the fifteenth, they acted ugly. Most of them wear guns, and they were in the store, threatening to shoot up the place unless they got their full pay.

'In the mêlée, a couple of men got to quarrelling and one

of them hit the other over the head with the weight from the scales. He dropped like a struck ox, and when they dragged him out into the air they couldn't bring him back to his senses.

'So the crowd started out with a rope, after the man that hit him. They trailed him easy enough into the slough, and then they couldn't find him in the high grass. They threshed around looking for him through that slough grass taller than their heads, till I guess they'd ruined any trail he'd left.

'They kept on hunting him till past noon, and lucky for him they didn't find him. When they got back to the store, the door was locked. They couldn't get in. Somebody had loaded the hurt man into a wagon and headed back East to look for a doctor.

'By this time men were piling into the place from all the other camps. They ate everything they could get hold of in the boarding shanty and most of them were drinking. They kept pounding on the store door and yelling to the paymaster to open up and pay them, but nobody answered.

'A crowd of near a thousand drunken men is an ugly thing to deal with. Somebody caught sight of that rope and shouted, "Hang the paymaster!" The whole crowd took it up and kept on yelling, "Hang him! Hang him!"

'A couple of men got on top of the lean-to roof and tore a hole in the shingles. They left the end of the rope dangling over the edge of the roof and the crowd grabbed hold of it. The two fellows dropped down on to the paymaster and got the noose around his neck.'

'Stop, Charles. The girls are awake,' said Ma.

'Pshaw, that's all there is to it,' Pa said. 'They hauled him up once or twice, is all. He gave in.'

'They didn't hang him?'

'Not enough to hurt much. Some of the crowd was breaking down the store door with neck-yokes, and the

storekeeper opened it. One of the fellows in the office cut
the rope and let the paymaster down, and opened up the
pay-window and the paymaster paid every man what he
claimed was due him. A good many men from the other
camps crowded in and drew pay, too. There wasn't any
bothering with time-checks.'

'Shame on him!' Laura cried out. Pa drew back the curtain. 'What did he do it for? I wouldn't! I wouldn't!' she
went on, before Pa or Ma could say a word. There she was,
sitting up on her knees in bed, her fists clenched.

'You wouldn't what?' said Pa.

'Pay them! They couldn't make me! They didn't make
you!'

'That mob was bigger than ours. And the paymaster
didn't have Big Jerry to help him,' said Pa.

'But you wouldn't have, Pa,' Laura said.

'Sh!' Ma hushed them. 'You'll wake Grace. I'm thankful
the paymaster was sensible. Better a live dog than a dead
lion.'

'Oh, no, Ma! You don't mean that!' Laura whispered.

'Anyway, discretion is the better part of valour. You
girls go to sleep,' Ma murmured.

'Please, Ma,' Mary whispered. 'How could he pay
them? Where did he get the money, when he'd already
paid out what he had?'

'That's so, where did he?' Ma asked.

'From the store. It's a big store and it had already taken
in most of what the men had been paid; they spend as fast
as they get,' said Pa. 'Now mind your Ma, girls, and go to
sleep.' He let the curtain fall.

Very softly under the quilt Mary and Laura talked until
Ma blew out the lamp. Mary said she wanted to go back to
Plum Creek. Laura did not answer that. She liked to feel
the great wild prairie all around the little shanty. Her heart
beat strong and fast; she could hear in her mind again the

savage fierce sound of that crowd's growl and Pa's cold voice saying, 'Don't crowd too close.' And she remembered the sweating men and sweating horses moving strongly through clouds of dust, building the railroad in a kind of song. She did not want ever to go back to Plum Creek.

CHAPTER 12

WINGS OVER SILVER LAKE

THE weather grew colder and the sky was full of wings and great birds flying. From east to west, from north to south, and as far up into the blue sky as eyes could see, were birds and birds and birds sailing on beating wings.

At evening down they came endlessly from the sky, sliding down long slopes of air to rest on the water of Silver Lake.

There were great, grey geese. There were smaller, snow-white brant that looked like snow at the water's edge. There were ducks of many kinds; the large mallards with a shimmering of purple and green on their wings, the red-heads, the bluebells, the canvasbacks, and teals and many others whose names Pa did not know. There were herons, and pelicans, and cranes. There were little mud-hens, and the small hell-divers that peppered the water thickly with their little black bodies. When a shot cracked, hell-divers up-ended and vanished quicker than winking. They went far down in the water and stayed there a long time.

At sunset the whole large lake was covered with birds of all kinds speaking in every kind of bird's voice to each other before they went to sleep for a night of rest on their long journey from north to south. The winter was driving them; the winter was coming behind them from the north. They knew it and started early so that they could rest on the way. All night they rested, comfortable on the water that held them so softly, and when dawn came, up they rose again to swim onward in the high air with their rested, strong wings.

One day Pa came from hunting, bringing a great, snow-white bird.

'I'm sorry, Caroline,' he said soberly. 'I would not have done it if I'd known. I've shot a swan. It was too beautiful to kill. But I had no idea it was a swan. I never saw one flying before.'

'It can't be helped now, Charles,' Ma told him. They all stood looking sorrowfully at the beautiful snowy bird that would never fly again. 'Come,' said Ma. 'I'll pluck its feathers and you skin it. We'll cure the skin with the swan's-down on.'

'It's bigger than I am,' Carrie said. The swan was so large that Pa measured it. Its feathery white wings measured eight feet from tip to tip.

Another day Pa brought a pelican to the shanty to show Ma what it was like. He opened the long bill and dead fish fell out of the pouch of skin underneath it. Ma snatched up her apron and pressed it to her face, and Carrie and Grace held their noses.

'Take it away, Charles, quick!' said Ma through the apron. Some of those fish were fresh, and some were fish that had been dead a long, long time. Pelicans were not fit to eat. Even their feathers smelled so strongly of rotten fish that Ma could not save them for pillows.

Pa shot all the ducks and geese that they could eat, but he shot nothing else except hawks. Sometimes he shot a hawk because hawks kill other birds. Every day Laura and Ma plucked feathers from the scalded skins of the ducks and geese that Pa shot for dinner.

'We'll soon have enough for another feather bed,' said Ma. 'Then you and Mary can sleep in feathers this winter.'

All those golden autumn days the sky was full of wings. Wings beating low over the blue water of Silver Lake, wings beating high in the blue air far above it. Wings of geese, of brant, of ducks and pelicans and cranes and heron and swans and gulls, bearing them all away to green fields in the South.

The wings and the golden weather and the tang of frost in the mornings made Laura want to go somewhere. She did not know where. She wanted only to go.

'Let's go West,' she said one night after supper. 'Pa, can't we go West when Uncle Henry does?'

Uncle Henry and Louisa and Charley had earned money enough to go West. They were going back to the Big Woods to sell their farm, and in the spring, with Aunt Polly, they were all driving West to Montana.

'Why can't we?' Laura said. 'There's all the money you've earned, Pa; three hundred dollars. And we've got the team and wagon. Oh, Pa, let's go on West!'

'Mercy, Laura!' Ma said. 'Whatever —' She could not go on.

'I know, little Half-pint,' said Pa, and his voice was very kind. 'You and I want to fly like the birds. But long ago I promised your Ma that you girls should go to school. You can't go to school and go West. When this town is built there'll be a school here. I'm going to get a homestead, Laura, and you girls are going to school.'

Laura looked at Ma, and then again at Pa, and she saw that it must happen; Pa would stay on a homestead, and she would go to school.

'You'll thank me some day, Laura. And you too, Charles,' Ma said gently.

'Just so you're content, Caroline, I'm satisfied,' said Pa. That was true, but he did want to go West. Laura turned back to the dish-pan and went on washing the supper dishes.

'Another thing, Laura,' said Pa. 'You know Ma was a teacher, and her mother before her. Ma's heart is set on one of you girls teaching school, and I guess it will have to be you. So you see you must have your schooling.'

Laura's heart jerked, and then she seemed to feel it falling, far, far down. She did not say anything. She knew that Pa and Ma, and Mary too, had thought that Mary would be a teacher. Now Mary couldn't teach, and – 'Oh, I won't! I won't!' Laura thought. 'I don't want to! I can't.' Then she said to herself, 'You must.'

She could not disappoint Ma. She must do as Pa said. So she had to be a school-teacher when she grew up. Besides, there was nothing else she could do to earn money.

CHAPTER 13

BREAKING CAMP

NOW all the vast, low earth rippled softly in gentle colours
under a faded sky. Grasses were golden-stemmed, and over
the prairie they spread a coverlet of buff and tan and brown
and warm brownish grey; only the sloughs were darker
with green. The birds were fewer, and hurrying. Often at
sunset a long flock talked anxiously, high above Silver Lake,
and instead of sinking to eat and rest on the water that must
have tempted them so much, the tired leader fell back,

another took his place, and they went on flying southward. Winter's cold was not far behind them and they could not pause to rest.

In the frosty mornings and the chilly evenings when they went to milk the cows, Laura and Lena wore shawls snug over their heads and pinned under their chins. Their bare legs were cold and the wind nipped their noses, but when they squatted down to milk the warm cows, the shawls covered them cosily and their feet warmed under them. And they sang while they milked.

> 'Where are you going, my pretty maid?
> I'm going a-milking, sir, she said.
> May I go with you, my pretty maid?
> Oh, yes, if you please, kind sir, she said.

> 'What is your fortune, my pretty maid?
> My face is my fortune, sir, she said.
> Then I can't marry you, my pretty maid.
> Nobody asked you, sir, she said.'

'Well, I guess we won't be seeing each other again for a long time,' Lena said one evening. The grading job at Silver Lake was nearly finished. Next morning early, Lena and Jean and Aunt Docia were leaving. They were going away before sun-up because they were getting away with three big wagonloads of goods from the company's stores. They would not tell anybody where they were going, for fear the company would catch them.

'I wish we'd had time to ride the black ponies again,' Laura said.

'Gosh!' Lena spoke that wicked word boldly, 'I'm glad this summer's over! I hate houses.' She swung the milk pail and chanted. 'No more cooking, no more dishes, no more washing, no more scrubbing! Whoop-ee!' Then she said, 'Well, good-bye. I guess you're going to stay right here as long as you live.'

'I guess so,' Laura said miserably. She was sure that Lena was going out West. Maybe even to Oregon. 'Well, good-bye.'

Next morning Laura milked the lone cow by her lonely self. Aunt Docia had driven away with a load of oats from the feed room. Lena had driven a wagonload of goods from the store, and Jean still another big load of scrapers and ploughs. Uncle Hi would follow them as soon as he settled with the company.

'I guess Hi's debt is big enough this time with all those goods charged to him,' Pa said.

'Shouldn't you have stopped it, Charles?' Ma worried.

'It's not my look-out,' said Pa. 'My orders were to let the contractor take anything he wanted, and charge it to him. Oh, come, Caroline! It wasn't stealing. Hi hasn't got away with any more than's due him for his work here and at the camp on the Sioux. The company cheated him there, and he's got even here. That's all there is to it.'

'Well,' Ma sighed, 'I'll be glad when these camps are gone and we're settled again.'

Every day the camp was noisy with men drawing their last pay and leaving. Wagon after wagon went away to the east. Every night the camp was emptier. One day Uncle Henry, Louisa and Charley started the long drive back to Wisconsin, to sell the farm. The boarding shanty and the bunkhouse were deserted, the store was empty, and Pa was only waiting till the company man came to check his book-keeping.

'We'll have to go East somewhere to spend the winter,' he said to Ma. 'This shanty's too thin for zero weather, even if the company'd let us stay in it, and even if we had any coal.'

'Oh, Charles,' Ma said, 'you haven't even found the homestead yet, and if we have to spend the money you've earned, just living till spring –'

'I know. But what can we do?' said Pa. 'I can find the homestead all right before we leave, and file on it next spring. Maybe next summer I can get a job to live on and pay for the lumber to build us a shanty. I could make a sod shanty, but even so it will take all we've got to live till spring, with the prices of supplies out here, and coal. No, we'd better go East for the winter.'

It was so hard to get ahead. Laura tried to cheer up, but she couldn't. She did not want to go back East again. She hated to leave Silver Lake to go East. They had got as far as Silver Lake and she wanted to hang on there, not to be pushed back. But if they must be, they must; next spring they could start again. It would do no good to complain.

'Don't you feel well, Laura?' Ma asked her.

'Oh, yes, Ma!' she answered. But she felt so heavy and dark that trying to be cheerful only made her more miserable.

The company man had come to check Pa's book-keeping, and the last wagons from the West were going by. Even the lake was almost empty of birds and the sky was bare, except for one hurrying streak of flyers. Ma and Laura mended the wagon-cover and baked bread for the long drive.

That evening Pa came whistling from the store, and blew into the shanty like a breeze.

'How'd you like to stay here all winter, Caroline?' he sang out, 'in the surveyors' house!'

'Oh, Pa! Can we?' Laura cried.

'You bet we can!' said Pa. 'If your Ma wants to. It's a good, sound, weather-tight house, Caroline. The head surveyor was at the store just now, and he says they thought they had to stay and they laid on coal and provisions enough to last them through, but if I'll take charge and be responsible for the company tools till spring, they'll go out for the winter. The company man's agreed.

'There's flour and beans and salt meat and potatoes, and

even some canned stuff, he told me. And coal. We can have the whole of it for nothing, just for staying out here this winter. We can use the stable for the cow and team. I told him I'd let him know early tomorrow morning. What do you say, Caroline?'

They all looked at Ma and waited. Laura could hardly keep still in her excitement. To stay at Silver Lake! Not to have to go back East, after all! Ma was disappointed; she had been wanting to go back to settled country. But she said, 'It does seem Providential, Charles. There's coal, you say?'

'I wouldn't think of staying without it,' said Pa. 'But the coal's there.'

'Well, supper's on the table,' said Ma. 'Wash up and eat before it gets cold. It does look like a good chance, Charles.'

At supper they talked of nothing else. It would be pleasant to live in a snug house; the shanty was cold with wind blowing through its cracks, though the door was shut and a fire was in the stove.

'Don't it make you feel rich –' Laura began.

'Doesn't,' said Ma.

'Doesn't it make you feel rich, Ma, just to think of the whole winter's provisions laid in, already?' said Laura.

'Not a penny going out till spring,' said Pa.

'Yes, Laura, it does,' Ma smiled. 'You're right, Charles, of course; we must stay.'

'Well, I don't know, Caroline,' Pa said. 'In some ways maybe we'd better not. So far as I know, we won't have a neighbour nearer than Brookins. That's sixty miles. If anything happened –'

A knock at the door startled them all. In answer to Pa's 'Come in!' a big man opened the door. He was bundled in thick coats and a muffler. His short beard was black, his cheeks were red, and his eyes were as black as the eyes of the little papoose in Indian territory whom Laura had never forgotten.

'Hullo, Boast!' Pa said. 'Come up to the fire; it's chilly tonight. This is my wife and girls. Mr Boast has filed on a homestead out here, and he's been working on the grade.'

Ma gave Mr Boast a chair by the fire and he held his hands out to the warmth. One hand was bandaged. 'Did you hurt your hand?' Ma asked kindly.

'Only a sprain,' said Mr Boast, 'but the heat feels good on it.' Turning to Pa he went on, 'I'm needing some help, Ingalls. You remember my team that I sold Pete? He paid me part down and said he'd pay the rest next payday. But he's kept putting it off, and now I'm darned if he hasn't skipped out with the team. I'd go after him and take them, but his son's with him and they'd put up a fight. I don't want trouble with two roughs at once, and me with a lame hand.'

'There's enough of us around yet to tend to it,' said Pa.

'I don't mean that,' said Mr Boast, 'I don't want any trouble.'

'Then just where do I come in?' Pa asked.

'I was thinking. There's no law out here, no way to collect a debt, no officers, not even a county. But maybe Pete don't know that.'

'Oho!' said Pa. 'You want me to make out some papers to serve on him?'

'I've got a man that'll act as sheriff and serve them,' Mr Boast said. His eyes twinkled as much as Pa's, but the twinkles were not alike. Mr Boast's eyes twinkled small and black, Pa's twinkled wide and blue.

Pa laughed out loud and slapped his knee. 'What a joke! Lucky I've got some legal foolscap left. I'll make out your papers, Boast! Go get your sheriff.'

Mr Boast hurried away while Ma and Laura hastily

cleared the table. Pa squared up to it and wrote on a large sheet of paper, red-lined down the sides.

'There!' he said finally, 'that looks important. And finished just in time.'

Mr Boast was knocking at the door. Another man was with him, wrapped in a big overcoat, a cap pulled low over his eyes and a muffler wrapped around his neck and across his mouth.

'Here you are, Sheriff!' Pa said to him. 'Serve this writ of attachment and bring back the team or the money, dead or alive, with costs of this suit at law!' Their laughter seemed to shake the shanty.

Pa looked at the cap and muffler that hid the man's face. 'Lucky for you it's a cold night, Sheriff!' he said.

When the two men shut the door behind them, and Pa stopped laughing, he said to Ma, 'That was the head surveyor, or I'll eat my hat!' He slapped his thigh and roared again.

In the night Mr Boast's voice and Pa's woke Laura. At the door Mr Boast was saying, 'I saw your light and stopped by to tell you it worked. Pete was so scared he'd have turned over the money and the team both. That crook's got reason to be scared of the law. Here are the costs, Ingalls. The surveyor wouldn't take any; he said the fun of it more than paid him.'

'You keep his share,' said Pa. 'I'll take mine. The dignity of this court must be upheld!'

When Mr Boast laughed, Laura and Mary and Carrie and Ma all burst out laughing. They couldn't help it. Pa's laugh was like great bells ringing; it made you feel warm and happy. But Mr Boast's laugh made everybody laugh.

'Hush, you'll wake Grace,' Ma said.

'What's the joke?' Carrie asked. She had been asleep and had only heard Mr Boast laugh.

'What are you laughing at?' Mary asked her.

'Mr Boast's laugh tickles,' Carrie said.

In the morning Mr Boast came to breakfast. The camp was gone and there was nowhere else to eat. The surveyors started East that morning in their buggy, and the last teamster passed. Mr Boast was the last man to go; he had had to wait until his hand was better so that he could drive his team. His hand was worse that morning because it had been chilled in the night, but he started East anyway. He was going to Iowa to be married.

'If you folks are going to stay here all winter, I don't know but I'll bring Ellie back and stay too,' he said, 'if we can make it before winter sets in.'

'Be glad to have you, Boast,' said Pa. Ma said, 'We would, indeed.'

Then they watched Mr Boast's wagon going, and heard its rattling die away on the wagon track to the East.

The whole prairie was empty now and not even one flock of birds was in the cold sky.

As soon as Mr Boast's wagon was out of sight, Pa brought his team and wagon to the door.

'Come, Caroline!' he called. 'Nobody's left in camp but us, and this is moving day!'

CHAPTER 14

THE SURVEYORS' HOUSE

THERE was no need to pack anything, for the surveyors'
house stood on the north shore of the lake not half a mile
from the shanty. Laura could hardly wait to see it. When
she had helped to put everything neatly into the wagon, and
Mary and Carrie and Ma and Grace were in it, Laura said
to Pa, 'Please, can't I run ahead?'

'"May," Laura,' Ma said. 'Really, Charles, don't you
think –'

'Nothing can hurt her,' Pa said. 'We'll have her in sight all the way. Follow the lake shore, Flutterbudget, and don't worry, Caroline; we'll be there in two shakes of a lamb's tail.'

So Laura ran ahead. Straight against the steady wind she ran. Her shawl flapped in the wind behind her and the cold of the wind poured through her. She felt her blood thin and chill in the wind, and then she felt it warm and pulsing strong, and her breath throbbed hard in her chest.

She passed the spoiled spots where the camp had been. The earth was hard under her pounding feet, and rough with dead grass. No one else was anywhere near. Everybody had gone now. The prairie, the whole vast prairie, and the great sky and the wind were clear and free.

Even the wagon was left behind now. But it was coming. Laura looked back, and Pa waved to her. When she stopped running she could hear the sound of the wind in the grasses and the lippety-lapping of the lake water. She hoppity-skipped on the short dry grass along the shore. She could shout if she wanted to. No one else was there. She shouted, 'It's ours! All ours!'

The shout seemed loud in her throat, but in the air it was thin. The wind took it away perhaps. Or the stillness of the empty land and sky would not be disturbed.

The surveyors' boots had worn a path through the grasses. It was smooth and soft to Laura's feet. She bent her shawled head to the wind and padded along the path, hurrying. It would be fun to see the surveyors' house all by herself.

It stood up in front of her suddenly. It was a big house, a real house with two stories, and glass windows. Its up-and-down boards were weathering from yellow to grey, and every crack was battened, as Pa had said. The door had a china knob. It opened into the lean-to over the back door.

Laura opened the door and peeped in. Then she pushed the door back, along the curved mark it had worn in the board floor, and she went in. This house had board floors; not as comfortable to bare feet as the earth floor of the shanty, but not so much work to keep clean.

The largeness of the empty house seemed to wait and listen. It seemed to know that Laura was there, but it had not made up its mind about her. It would wait and see. Against its walls the wind made a lonely sound, but that was outside the house. She tiptoed across the lean-to and opened a door on its farther side.

Laura looked at the large front room. Its board walls were still yellow inside, and sunshine from its west window slanted yellow on the floor. A cool light came in from the window to the east beside the front door. The surveyors had left their stove! It was a larger stove than the one that Ma had brought from Plum Creek; it had six lids on top and two oven doors, and it stood all set up with its stove-pipe in place.

Spaced on the wall beyond it were three doors. All of them were shut.

Laura tiptoed across the wide floor, and softly opened one door. There was a small room, with a bedstead in it. This room had a window, too.

Softly Laura opened the middle door. She was surprised. Steeply up in front of her went a stair, just the width of the door. She looked up, and saw the underside of a slanting roof high overhead. She went up a few steps, and a big attic opened out on both sides of the stairs. It was twice as big as the large room downstairs. A window in each gable end lighted the whole empty place under the roof.

That made three rooms already, and still there was another door. Laura thought that there must have been a great many surveyors to need so much space. This would be by far the largest house she had ever lived in.

She opened the third door. A squeal of excitement came out of her mouth and startled the listening house. There before her eyes was a little store. All up the walls of that small room were shelves, and on the shelves were dishes, and pans and pots, and boxes, and cans. All around under the shelves stood barrels and boxes.

The first barrel was nearly full of flour. The second held corn meal. The third had a tight lid, and it was full of pieces of fat, white pork held down in brown brine. Laura had never seen so much salt pork at one time. There was a wooden box full of square soda crackers, and a box full of big slabs of salted fish. There was a large box of dried apples, and two sacks full of potatoes, and another big sack nearly full of beans.

The wagon was at the door. Laura ran out, shouting, 'Oh, Ma, come quick and see! There's so many things – And a big attic, Mary! And a stove, and crackers, soda crackers!'

Ma looked at everything and she was pleased. 'It's very nice, I'm sure,' she said. 'And so clean. We can get settled here in a jiffy. Bring me the broom, Carrie.'

Pa didn't even have to set up a stove. He put Ma's stove in the lean-to outside the back door, where the coal was. Then while Pa built a fire they arranged the table and chairs in the large front room. Ma set Mary's rocking-chair by the open oven door. Already that good stove was giving off heat, and in the warm corner Mary sat holding Grace and amusing her, to keep her out of the way while Ma and Laura and Carrie were busy.

Ma made the big bed on the bedstead in the bedroom. She hung her clothes and Pa's on nails in the wall there, and covered them neatly with a sheet. Upstairs in the large, low attic Laura and Carrie made two neat beds on the bedsteads there, one for Carrie and the other for Laura and Mary. Then they carried their clothes and their boxes upstairs; they hung the clothes on the gable wall by one window, and under it they set their boxes.

Everything was neat now, so they went downstairs to help Ma get supper. Pa came in bringing a large, shallow packing box.

'What's that for, Charles?' Ma asked, and Pa said, 'This is Grace's trundle bed!'

'It's the only thing we needed!' Ma exclaimed.

'The sides are high enough to hold her covers tucked in,' said Pa.

'And low enough to go under our bed in the day-time, like any trundle bed,' said Ma.

Laura and Carrie made up a little bed for Grace in the packing box, and slid it under the big bed, and pulled it out again for the night. The moving-in was done.

Supper was a feast. The surveyors' pretty dishes made the table gay. Little sour cucumber pickles, from a jar the surveyors had left, made the warmed-up roast duck and fried potatoes taste different. And after they were eaten, Ma stepped into the pantry and brought out – 'Guess what?' she said.

She set before each of them a little dish of canned peaches, and two soda crackers! 'We'll have a treat,' she said, 'to celebrate living in a house again.'

It was fine to be eating in such a large place, with a board floor, and the glass windows glittering black against the night outside. Slowly, slowly they ate the smooth, cool peaches and the sweet golden juice, and carefully licked their spoons.

Then the dishes were quickly cleared away and washed in the handy pantry. The table's leaves were dropped, the red-and-white checked cloth spread, and the bright-shining lamp set on its centre. Ma settled with Grace in the rocking-chair, and Pa said, 'This makes a fellow feel like music. Bring me the fiddle box, Laura!'

He tightened and tuned the strings and rosined the bow. Winter evenings were coming again when Pa played the fiddle. He looked around contentedly at them all and at the good walls that would keep them comfortable.

'I must manage something for curtains,' Ma said.

Pa paused with the bow poised above the fiddle. 'Don't you realize, Caroline, that our nearest neighbour to the east is sixty miles away and our nearest west is forty miles? When winter shuts down, they might as well be farther off. We've got the world to ourselves! I saw only one flock of wild geese today, flying high and fast. They weren't stopping at any lakes; not they! They were hurrying south. Looked to me like the last flock of the season. So even the geese have left us.'

His fiddle bow touched the strings and he began to play. Softly Laura began to sing:

> 'One night when the winds blew bitter,
> Blew bitter across the wild moor,
> Young Mary she came with her child,
> Wandering home to her own father's door,
> Crying, Father, O pray let me in!
> Take pity on me I implore
> Or the child in my arms will die
> From the winds that blow across the wild moor.
>
> But her father was deaf to her cries
> Not a voice nor a sound reached the door
> But the watch dogs did howl
> And the village bells tolled
> And the winds blew across the –'

Pa stopped. 'That song doesn't fit!' he exclaimed. 'What was I thinking of! Now here's something worth singing.'

Merrily the fiddle sang and Pa sang with it. Laura and Mary and Carrie sang too, with all their might.

> 'I've travelled about a bit in my time
> And of troubles I've seen a few
> But found it better in every clime
> To paddle my own canoe.
>
> My wants are few. I care not at all
> If my debts are paid when due.
> I drive away strife in the ocean of life
> While I paddle my own canoe.
>
> Then love your neighbour as yourself
> As the world you go travelling through
> And never sit down with a tear or a frown
> But paddle your own canoe!'

'That's what we'll be doing this winter,' said Pa. 'And we've done it a good many times before. Haven't we, Caroline?'

'Yes, Charles,' Ma agreed. 'And we haven't always been so comfortable and so well provided for.'

'Everything snug as bugs in a rug,' said Pa, tuning the fiddle. 'I piled bags of oats across one end of the stable to make a small place for the cow and the team. They'll have all they can eat, too, and they'll be warm and cosy. Yes, we've got everything to be thankful for.'

Then he played the fiddle again. He played on and on, jigs and reels and hornpipes and marches. Ma laid Grace in her little trundle bed and shut the door. Then she sat idly rocking, listening to the music. Ma and Mary and Laura and Carrie listened until they were full, full of music. No one spoke of bed-time, because this was their first evening in the new house, all by themselves on the prairie.

At last Pa laid the fiddle and the bow in the fiddle box. As he shut down the lid, a long, mournful, lonely howl came from the night outside the window. Very near, it was.

Laura sprang to her feet. Ma rushed to comfort Grace's

screaming in the bedroom. Carrie sat frozen white, with big, round eyes.

'It's – it's only a wolf, Carrie,' Laura said.

'There, there!' said Pa. 'A fellow'd think you'd never heard a wolf before. Yes, Caroline, the stable door is well fastened.'

CHAPTER 15

THE LAST MAN OUT

NEXT morning the sun shone but the wind was colder and there was a feeling of storm in the air. Pa had come from doing the chores and was warming his hands by the stove, while Ma and Laura put breakfast on the table, when they heard a wagon rattling.

It stopped by the front door. The driver shouted and Pa went out to him. Through the window Laura saw them talking in the cold wind.

In a moment Pa came back and hurriedly put on his overcoat and his mittens while he said, 'We've got a neighbour I didn't know about last night. An old man, sick and all alone. I'm going out there now, I'll tell you all about it when I get back.'

He drove away with the stranger and it was some time before he came walking home.

'Brrrr! It's getting colder,' he said, dropping his coat

and mittens on a chair and bending over the stove to warm himself before he unwound his muffler. 'Well, it's a good job done.

'That teamster's the last one out. He came all the way from the Jim River and didn't find a soul. Everyone along the line is going. Last night, when dark caught him, he saw a light about two miles north of the grade and drove to it on the chance of finding a place to stay all night.

'Well, Caroline, he found a claim shanty and an old man all by himself. His name is Woodworth. He has consumption, and came out here to take the prairie-climate cure. He's been living on his claim all summer and was going to stay all winter.

'Well, he's so feeble, the teamster tried to get him to go out. Told him it's his last chance, but Woodworth wouldn't go. So when the teamster saw our smoke this morning, he stopped to see if he couldn't get somebody to help him persuade the old man.

'Caroline, he was skin and bones. But bound and determined to stick to the prairie cure. Said it was the one cure the doctors recommended as pretty near a sure-fire thing.'

'Folks come from all over the world to take it,' said Ma.

'Yes, I know, Caroline. It's true enough, I guess, these prairies are about the only thing that cures consumption. But if you'd seen him, Caroline. No, he wasn't in any shape to stay alone in a claim shanty, fifteen miles from a neighbour. The place for him is with his own folks.

'Anyhow, the teamster and I packed him up and loaded him and his things into the wagon. Lifted him in, as easy as if he was Carrie, here. In the end he was glad to be going. He'll be a sight more comfortable with his folks in the East.'

'He'll near freeze to death, riding in a wagon this cold day,' Ma said, putting more coal on the fire.

'He's dressed warmly, wearing a good overcoat. We wrapped him in blankets besides and heated a bag of oats for his feet. He'll make it all right. That teamster is one fine fellow.'

Thinking of that old man going out with the last teamster, Laura really knew how deserted the country was. It would take them two long days to get to the Big Sioux River. All the way between the Big Sioux and the Jim, there was nobody at all except them, there in the surveyors' house.

'Pa, did you see wolf tracks this morning?' Laura asked.

'Yes, plenty of them, all around the stable,' said Pa. 'Big tracks too. Must be buffalo wolves. But they couldn't get in. All the birds have gone south, and the antelope were scared away by the men working on the grade, so the wolves will have to move on too. They won't stay where they can't kill anything to eat.'

After breakfast he went to the stable, and as soon as the housework was done Laura put on her shawl and went too. She wanted to see the wolf tracks.

She had never seen such huge ones, and deep. Those wolves must be very big and heavy. 'Buffalo wolves are the largest wolves on the prairie and very fierce,' Pa told her. 'I'd hate to meet one without a gun.'

He was looking the stable over carefully, to see that every board was nailed fast. He drove in more nails, to make the walls solid, and he put an extra bolt on the door. 'If one gets broken, the other might hold,' he said.

Snow began to fall while Laura handed him nails and he hammered them in. The wind blew strong and keen, but it was a straight wind, not a blizzard wind. Still it was so cold that they could not talk.

At supper in the warm house Pa said, 'I don't believe the winters are going to be so bad out here. Seems like the blizzards sort of draw down through western Minnesota. We are farther west out here, and they say that three degrees west is as good as one degree south.'

After supper they all gathered in the warmth of the stove.

Ma rocked Grace slowly to and fro, and Laura brought Pa the fiddle box. Now the happy winter evenings were begun.

> 'Hail Columbia, happy land! (Pa sang with the fiddle)
> Hail, ye heroes, Heaven born band!
> Firm, united let us be,
> Rallying 'round our liberty,
> As a band of brothers joined
> Peace and safety we shall find.'

He looked at Mary sitting quietly with beautiful empty eyes and folded hands in her rocking-chair by the oven. 'What shall I play for you, Mary?'

'I would like to hear "Highland Mary", Pa.'

Softly Pa played a verse. 'Now, Mary! Help sing!' he said, and they sang together.

> 'How sweetly bloomed the gay, green birk,
> How rich the hawthorn's blossom,
> As underneath their fragrant shade
> I clasped her to my bosom.

> 'The golden hours on angel wings
> Flew o'er me and my dearie
> For dear to me as light and life
> Was my sweet Highland Mary!'

'It's sweet,' Mary said when the last note died away.

'It's sweet but it's sad,' said Laura. 'I like "Coming Through the Rye".'

'I'll play it,' Pa said, 'but I won't sing it alone. It isn't fair for me to do all the entertaining.'

So gaily all together they sang the lively song. And Laura got up and pretended to be wading across a creek, holding her skirts above her ankles and laughing back over her shoulder, singing:

> 'Ilka lassie has her laddie,
> Nane, they say, ha'e I,
> Yet all the lads they smile at me
> When coming through the Rye.'

Then Pa's fiddle twinkled short, gay little notes, and he sang:

> 'I'm Captain Jinks of the Horse Marines!
> I feed my horse on corn and beans,
> And I often go beyond my means
> To court the girls all in their teens,
> For I'm Captain Jinks of the Horse Marines,
> I'm Captain in the Army!'

Pa nodded at Laura, and she went on singing with the fiddle:

> 'I am Mrs Jinks of Madison Square,
> I wear fine clothes and I curl my hair,
> The Captain went on a regular tear
> And they kicked him out of the Army!

'Laura!' Ma said. 'Charles, do you think that is a nice song for a girl to sing?'

'She sang it well,' said Pa. 'Now, Carrie, you must do your share. Get out here with Laura and see what you can do.'

He showed them how to hold hands and step to the tune of a polka. Then he played it and they danced while he sang:

> 'First! the heel and then the toe,
> That's the way the steps do go,
> First the heel and then the toe,
> That's the way the steps do go,
> First-the-heel-and-then-the-toe –'

Faster and faster he played, and faster they danced, with higher and higher steps, back and forth and whirling back again till they were breathless and hot with dancing and laughing.

'Now then,' said Pa, 'try a bit of a waltz,' and the music flowed smoothly in gliding long waves. 'Just float on the music,' Pa sang to them softly. 'Just float on the music, glide smoothly and turn.'

Laura and Carrie waltzed across the room and back, and around and around the room, while Grace sat up in Ma's lap and watched them with round eyes and Mary listened quietly to the music and the dancing feet.

'That's fine, girls,' said Pa. 'We must have more of it this winter. You're growing up now and you must know how to dance. You're going to be fine dancers, both of you.'

'Oh, Pa, you aren't stopping!' Laura cried.

'It's long past bed-time,' said Pa. 'And there'll be plenty more long, cosy evenings before spring.'

Bitter cold came down the stairway when Laura opened the door. She hurried up the steps, carrying the lighted lantern, and behind her Mary and Carrie hurried. There was a little warmth around the stove-pipe that came up from the room below, and close to it they undressed and with shivering fingers pulled their nightgowns over their underflannels. Chattering, they crawled into their cold beds and Laura blew out the lantern.

In the dark she and Mary cuddled together, and slowly the blankets lost their chill. All around the house the black cold of the night was as high as the sky and as wide as the world, and there was nothing in it but the lonely wind.

'Mary,' Laura whispered. 'I guess the wolves have gone. I didn't hear them howl, did you?'

'I hope they have,' Mary answered drowsily.

CHAPTER 16

WINTER DAYS

THE weather grew colder. Silver Lake was frozen. Snow fell, but always the wind blew the ice clean, drifting the snow into the tall grass of the sloughs and driving it into waves on the low shores.

On the whole white prairie nothing moved but blowing snow, and the only sound in the vast silence was the sound of the wind.

In the snug house Laura and Carrie helped Ma with the housework, and Grace played, running about the big room with toddling short steps. Whenever she was tired of play she climbed into Mary's lap, for that was the warmest place and Mary would always tell her a story. Listening to stories, Grace would fall asleep. Then Ma laid her in her trundle bed by the stove, and they all settled down for a cosy afternoon of knitting and sewing and crocheting.

Pa did the chores and walked the trap-line he had set

along the edge of Big Slough. In the lean-to he skinned foxes and coyotes and muskrats, and stretched the furs on boards to dry.

The prairie was so desolate and the wind so cold that Mary did not go out at all. She loved to sit sewing in the pleasant, warm house, taking tiny, even stitches with the needle that Laura threaded for her.

At twilight Mary did not put away her sewing. She told Laura, 'I can sew when you can't see to, because I see with my fingers.'

'You sew more beautifully than I can, anytime,' Laura told her. 'You always could.'

Even Laura liked the cosy afternoons of rocking and stitching and talking a little, though she never would truly enjoy sewing as Mary did. Often she was restless in the house. Then she would walk from window to window, looking into a whirl of snowflakes and listening to the wind, till Ma said gently, 'I declare I don't know what gets into you, Laura.'

When the sun shone, no matter how cold it was, Laura must go out. When Ma would let them go, she and Carrie, well wrapped up in coats and hoods, with shoes and mittens and mufflers on, went sliding on Silver Lake. Holding hands, they ran a little way and then slid on the dark, smooth ice. First on one foot, then on the other, with little runs between slides, they went back and forth, breathless and warm and laughing.

Those were glorious days when they were out in the glitter of the sharp cold. Then it was good to come into the warm, close house, and good to eat supper, and through the evening of music and singing and dancing, Laura was the merriest of all.

One stormy day Pa brought a wide, square board in by the stove, and with his pencil he marked it off in small squares inside a plain border.

'Whatever are you making, Pa?' Laura asked, and he answered, 'Wait and see.'

He heated the tip of the poker red-hot in the stove, and carefully he burned black every alternate little square.

'Curiosity killed a cat, Pa,' Laura said.

'You look pretty healthy,' said Pa. Tantalizing, he sat there whittling until he had made twenty-four small squares of wood. Half of them he laid on the hot stove, turning them until they were burned black all over.

Then he ranged all these pieces in the squares on the board, and set the board on his knees.

'Now, Laura!' he said.

'Now what?' said Laura.

'These are checkers, and this is a checker board. Pull up your chair, and I'll show you how to play checkers.'

She learned so well that before that storm ended she had beaten Pa in one game. But after that, they did not play so immoderately. Ma did not care to play, nor Carrie, so after one game Pa always put the board away.

'Checkers is a selfish game,' he said, 'for only two can play it. Bring me the fiddle, Flutterbudget.'

CHAPTER 17

WOLVES ON SILVER LAKE

THERE came a night when moonlight shone silver clear.
The earth was endless white and the wind was still.

Beyond every window the white world stretched far
away in frosty glitter, and the sky was a curve of light.
Laura could not settle down to anything. She didn't want to
play games. She hardly heard even the music of Pa's fiddle.

She did not want to dance, but she felt that she must move swiftly. She must be going somewhere.

Suddenly she exclaimed, 'Carrie! Let's go slide on the ice!'

'In the night, Laura?' Ma was astonished.

'It's light outdoors,' Laura replied. 'Almost as light as day.'

'It will be all right, Caroline,' Pa said. 'There's nothing to hurt them, if they don't stay too long and freeze.'

So Ma told them, 'You may go for a quick run. Don't stay until you get too cold.'

Laura and Carrie hurried into their coats and hoods and mittens. Their shoes were new and the soles thick. Ma had knitted their woollen stockings, and their red flannel underclothes came down over their knees and buttoned in a snug band around each stocking. Their flannel petticoats were thick and warm, and their dresses and their coats were wool, and so were their hoods and mufflers.

Out of the warm house they burst into the breath-taking air that tingled with cold. They ran a race on the snowy path down the low hill to the stables. Then they followed the path that the horses and the cow had made when Pa led them through the snow to water at the hole he had cut in the lake ice.

'We mustn't go near the water hole,' Laura said, and she led Carrie along the lake shore until they were well away from it. Then they stopped and looked at the night.

It was so beautiful that they hardly breathed. The great round moon hung in the sky and its radiance poured over a silvery world. Far, far away in every direction stretched motionless flatness, softly shining as if it were made of soft light. In the midst lay the dark, smooth lake, and a glittering moonpath stretched across it. Tall grass stood up in black lines from the snow drifted in the sloughs.

The stable lay low and dark near the shore, and on the

low hill stood the dark, small, surveyors' house, with the yellow light in the window twinkling from its darkness.

'How still it is,' Carrie whispered. 'Listen how still it is.'

Laura's heart swelled. She felt herself a part of the wide land, of the far deep sky and the brilliant moonlight. She wanted to fly. But Carrie was little and almost afraid, so she took hold of Carrie's hand and said, 'Let's slide. Come on, run!'

With hands clasped, they ran a little way. Then with right foot first they slid on the smooth ice much farther than they had run.

'On the moonpath, Carrie! Let's follow the moonpath,' Laura cried.

And so they ran and slid, and ran and slid again, on the glittering moonpath into the light from the silver moon. Farther and farther from shore they went, straight towards the high bank on the other side.

They swooped and almost seemed to fly. If Carrie lost her balance, Laura held her up. If Laura was unsteady, Carrie's hand steadied her.

Close to the farther shore, almost in the shadow of the high bank, they stopped. Something made Laura look up to the top of the bank.

And there, dark against the moonlight, stood a great wolf!

He was looking towards her. The wind stirred his fur and the moonlight seemed to run in and out of it.

'Let's go back,' Laura said quickly, as she turned, taking Carrie with her. 'I can go faster than you.'

She ran and slid and ran again as fast as she could, but Carrie kept up.

'I saw it too,' Carrie panted. 'Was it a wolf?'

'Don't talk!' Laura answered. 'Hurry!'

Laura could hear their feet running and sliding on the ice.

She listened for a sound behind them, but there was none. Then they ran and slid without a word until they came to the path by the water-hole. As they ran up the path, Laura looked back but she could see nothing on the lake nor on the bank beyond.

Laura and Carrie didn't stop running. They ran up the hill to the house, opened the back door and ran into the lean-to. They ran across that, burst through the door into the front room and slammed it shut behind them. Then leaned against it, panting.

Pa sprang to his feet, 'What is it?' he asked. 'What has frightened you?'

'Was it a wolf, Laura?' Carrie gasped.

'It was a wolf, Pa,' Laura gulped, catching her breath. 'A great, big wolf! And I was afraid Carrie couldn't run fast enough but she did.'

'I should say she did!' Pa exclaimed. 'Where is this wolf?'

'I don't know. It is gone,' Laura told him.

Ma helped them take off their wraps. 'Sit down and rest! You are all out of breath,' she said.

'Where was the wolf?' Pa wanted to know.

'Up on the bank,' Carrie said, and Laura added, 'The high bank across the lake.'

'Did you girls go clear there?' Pa asked in surprise. 'And ran all the way back after you saw him! I had no idea you would go so far. It is a good half-mile.'

'We followed the moonpath,' Laura told him. Pa looked at her strangely. 'You would!' he said. 'I thought those wolves had gone. It was careless of me. I'll hunt them tomorrow.'

Mary sat still, but her face was white. 'Oh, girls,' she almost whispered. 'Suppose he had caught you!'

Then they all sat silent while Laura and Carrie rested.

Laura was glad to be safe in the warm room with the

desolate prairie shut out. If anything had happened to Carrie, it would have been her fault for taking her so far across the lake.

But nothing had happened. She could almost see again the great wolf with the wind ruffling the moonlight on his fur.

'Pa!' she said in a low voice.

'Yes, Laura?' Pa answered.

'I hope you don't find the wolf, Pa,' Laura said.

'Why ever not?' Ma wondered.

'Because he didn't chase us,' Laura told her.

'He didn't chase us, Pa, and he could have caught us.'

A long, wild, wolf howl rose and faded away on the stillness.

Another answered it. Then silence again.

Laura's heart seemed to turn over with a sickening flop and she found herself on her feet. She was glad of Ma's steadying hand on her arm.

'Poor girl! You are nervous as a witch and no wonder,' Ma said softly.

Ma took a hot flat-iron from the back of the stove, wrapped it tightly in a cloth and gave it to Carrie.

'It is bedtime,' she said. 'Here is the hot iron for your feet.'

'And here is yours, Laura,' as she wrapped another. 'Be sure you put it in the middle of the bed so Mary's feet can reach it too.'

As Laura shut the stair door behind them, Pa was talking earnestly to Ma. But Laura could not hear what he said for the ringing in her ears.

CHAPTER 18

PA FINDS THE HOMESTEAD

AFTER breakfast next morning Pa took his gun and set out. All that morning Laura was listening for a shot and not wanting to hear it. All morning she remembered the great wolf sitting quiet in the moonlight that shimmered through his thick fur.

Pa was late for dinner. It was long past noon when he stamped the snow from his feet in the lean-to. He came in and put his gun on the wall, and hung his cap and coat on their nail. His mittens he hung, by their thumbs, to dry on the line behind the stove. Then he washed his face and hands in the tin basin on the bench, and before the small glass that hung above it he combed his hair and his beard.

'Sorry I kept dinner waiting, Caroline,' he said. 'I was gone longer than I thought. Went farther than I intended.'

'It doesn't matter, Charles; I've kept dinner warm,' Ma replied. 'Come to the table, girls! Don't keep Pa waiting.'

'How far did you go, Pa?' Mary asked.

'Better than ten miles, all told,' said Pa. 'Those wolf tracks led me a chase.'

'Did you get the wolf, Pa?' Carrie wanted to know. Laura did not say anything.

Pa smiled at Carrie and said, 'Now, now, don't ask questions. I'll tell you all about it. I went across the lake, followed the marks you girls made last night. And what do you suppose I found in that high bank where you saw the wolf?'

'You found the wolf,' Carrie said confidently. Laura still said nothing. Her food was choking her; she could hardly swallow the smallest mouthful.

'I found the wolves' *den*,' said Pa. 'And the biggest wolves' tracks I ever saw. Girls, there were two big buffalo wolves at that den last night.'

Mary and Carrie gasped. Ma said, 'Charles!'

'It's too late to be scared now,' Pa told them. 'But that's what you girls did. You went right up to the wolves' den and there were the wolves.

'Their tracks were fresh, and all the signs show plain as day what they were doing. It's an old den, and from their size they're no young wolves. I'd say they'd been living there for some years. But they haven't been living there this winter.

'They came down from the north-west some time yesterday evening and went pretty straight to that den. They stayed around it, in and out of it, maybe till this morning. I followed their tracks from there, down along Big Slough and out on the prairie, south-west.

'From the time they left the old den, those wolves never stopped. They trotted along, side by side, as if they had started on a long journey and knew where they were going.

I followed them far enough to be sure that I couldn't get a shot at them. They've left for good.'

Laura took a deep breath as though she had forgotten to breathe till now. Pa looked at her. 'You are glad they got away, Laura?' he asked.

'Yes, Pa, I am,' Laura answered. 'They didn't chase us.'

'No, Laura, they didn't chase you. And for the life of me, I can't figure out why they didn't.'

'And what were they doing at that old den?' Ma wondered.

'They were just looking at it,' said Pa. 'My belief is they came back to visit the old place where they lived before the graders came in and the antelope left. Maybe they used to live here before the hunters killed the last buffalo. Buffalo wolves were all over this country once, but there's not many left now, even around here. The railroads and settlements kept driving them farther West. One thing's certain if I know anything about wild animal tracks; those two wolves came straight from the West and went straight back West, and all they did here was to stop one night at the old den. And I wouldn't wonder if they're pretty nearly the last buffalo wolves that'll ever be seen in this part of the country.'

'Oh, Pa, the poor wolves,' Laura mourned.

'Mercy on us,' Ma said briskly. 'There's enough to be sorry for, without being sorry for the feelings of wild beasts! Be thankful the brutes didn't do any worse than scare you girls last night.'

'That isn't all, Caroline!' Pa announced. 'I've got some news. I've found our homestead.'

'Oh, where, Pa! What's it like? How far is it?' Mary and Laura and Carrie asked, excited. Ma said, 'That's good, Charles.'

Pa pushed back his plate, drank his tea, wiped his moustache, and said, 'It is just right in every way. It lies south of where the lake joins Big Slough, and the slough curves around to the west of it. There's a rise in the prairie to the south of the slough, that will make a nice place to build. A little hill just west of it crowds the slough back on that side. On the quarter section there's upland hay and plough land lying to the south; and good grazing on all of it, everything a farmer could ask for. And it's near the town-site, so the girls can go to school.'

'I'm glad, Charles,' said Ma.

'It's a funny thing,' Pa said. 'Here I've been looking around this country for months and never finding a quarter section that just exactly suited me. And that one was lying there all the time. Likely enough I wouldn't have come across it at all, if this wolf chase hadn't taken me across the lake and down along the slough on that side.'

'I wish you had filed on it last fall,' Ma worried.

'Nobody'll be in here this winter,' Pa said confidently. 'I'll get out to Brookins and file on that claim next spring before anybody else is looking for a homestead.'

CHAPTER 19

CHRISTMAS EVE

IT had snowed all day and soft, large flakes were still falling. The winds were quiet so that the snow lay deep on the ground, and Pa took the shovel with him when he went to do the evening chores.

'Well, it's a white Christmas,' he said.

'Yes, and we're all here and all well, so it's a merry one,' said Ma.

The surveyors' house was full of secrets. Mary had knitted new, warm socks for Pa's Christmas present. Laura had made him a necktie from a piece of silk she found in Ma's scrap bag. Together in the attic, she and Carrie had made an apron for Ma from one of the calico curtains that had hung in the shanty. In the scrap bag they found a piece of fine, white muslin; Laura had cut a small square from it, and secretly Mary had hemmed the square with her fine stitches and made a handkerchief for Ma. They put it in the apron pocket. Then they had wrapped the apron in tissue paper and hidden it under the quilt blocks in Mary's box.

There had been a blanket, striped across the ends in red and green. The blanket was worn out, but the striped end was good, and from it Ma had cut bed shoes for Mary. Laura had made one, and Carrie the other, seaming and turning and finishing them neatly with cords and tassels of yarn. The shoes were hidden carefully in Ma's bedroom so that Mary would not find them.

Laura and Mary had wanted to make mittens for Carrie, but they had not enough yarn. There was a little white yarn, and a little red, and a little blue, but not enough of any colour to make mittens.

'I know!' Mary said. 'We'll make the hands white, and the wrists in red and blue strips!' Every morning while Carrie was making her bed in the attic, Laura and Mary had knitted as fast as they could; when they heard her coming downstairs, they hid the mittens in Mary's knitting basket. The mittens were there now, finished.

Grace's Christmas present was to be the most beautiful of all. They had all worked at it together in the warm room, for Grace was so little that she didn't notice.

Ma had taken the swan's skin from its careful wrappings, and cut from it a little hood. The skin was so delicate that Ma trusted no one else to handle that; she sewed every stitch of the hood herself. But she let Laura and Carrie piece out the lining, of scraps of blue silk from the scrap bag. After Ma sewed the swan's-down hood to the lining, it would not tear.

Then Ma looked again in the scrap bag, and chose a large piece of soft blue woollen cloth, that had once been her best winter dress. Out of it she cut a little coat. Laura and Carrie sewed the seams and pressed them; Mary put the tiny stitches in the hem at the bottom. Then on the coat Ma sewed a collar of the soft swan's-down, and put narrow swan's-down cuffs on the sleeves.

The blue coat trimmed with the white swan's-down and the delicate swan's-down hood, with its lining as blue as Grace's eyes, were beautiful.

'It's like making doll's clothes,' Laura said.

'Grace will be lovelier than any doll,' Mary declared.

'Oh, let's put them on her now!' Carrie cried, dancing in her eagerness.

But Ma had said the coat and the hood must be laid away until Christmas, and they were. They were waiting now for tomorrow morning to come.

Pa had gone hunting. He said he intended to have the biggest jack rabbit in the territory for the Christmas dinner. And he had. At least, he had brought home the very biggest rabbit they had ever seen. Skinned and cleaned and frozen stiff, it waited now in the lean-to to be roasted tomorrow.

Pa came in from the stable, stamping the snow from his feet. He broke the ice from his moustache and spread his hands in the warmth above the stove.

'Whew!' he said. 'This is a humdinger of a cold spell for the night before Christmas. It's too cold for Santa Claus to be out,' and his eyes twinkled at Carrie.

'We don't need Santa Claus! We've all been –' Carrie began, then she clapped her hand over her mouth and looked quickly to see if Laura and Mary had noticed how nearly she had told secrets.

Pa turned around to warm his back in the heat from the oven, and he looked happily at them all.

'We're all snug under cover anyway,' he said. 'Ellen and Sam and David are warm and comfortable too, and I gave them an extra feed for Christmas Eve. Yes, it's a pretty good Christmas, isn't it, Caroline?'

'Yes, Charles, it is,' said Ma. She set the bowl of hot corn meal mush on the table, and poured out the milk. 'Come now, and eat. A hot supper will warm you quicker than anything else, Charles.'

At supper they talked about other Christmases. They had had so many Christmases together, and here they were again, all together and warm and fed and happy. Upstairs in Laura's box there was still Charlotte, the rag doll from her Christmas stocking in the Big Woods. The tin cups and the pennies from Christmas in Indian Territory were gone now, but Laura and Mary remembered Mr Edwards who had walked forty miles to Independence and back, to bring those presents from Santa Claus. They never had heard of Mr Edwards since he started alone down the Verdigris River, and they wondered what had become of him.

'Wherever he is, let's hope he's as lucky as we are,' said Pa. Wherever he was, they were remembering him and wishing him happiness.

'And you're here, Pa,' Laura said. 'You're not lost in a blizzard.' For a moment they all looked silently at Pa, thinking of that dreadful Christmas when he had not come home and they feared he never would.

Tears came into Ma's eyes. She tried to hide them, but she had to brush them away with her hand. They all pretended not to notice. 'It's just thankfulness, Charles,' Ma said, blowing her nose.

Then Pa burst out laughing. 'That was the joke on me!' he said. 'Starving to death for three days and nights, and eating the oyster crackers and the Christmas candy, and all the time I was under the bank of our own creek, not a hundred yards from the house!'

'I think the best Christmas was the time there was the Sunday-school Christmas Tree,' said Mary. 'You're too little to remember, Carrie, but Oh! how wonderful that was!'

'It wasn't really as good as this one,' Laura said. 'Because now Carrie is old enough to remember, and now we have Grace.' There was Carrie – the wolf didn't hurt her. And there on Ma's lap sat the littlest sister Grace, with her hair the colour of sunshine and eyes as blue as violets.

'Yes, this is best after all,' Mary decided. 'And maybe next year there'll be a Sunday school here.'

The mush was gone. Pa scraped the last drop of milk from his bowl and drank his tea. 'Well,' he said, 'we can't have a tree, for there isn't so much as a bush on Silver Lake. We wouldn't want one anyway, just for ourselves. But we can have a little Sunday-school celebration of our own, Mary.'

He went to get his fiddle box, and while Ma and Laura washed the bowls and the pot and set them away, he tuned the fiddle and rosined the bow.

Frost was thick on the window-panes and frost furred the cracks around the door. Thickly against the clear upper edges of the window-panes the snowflakes fluttered. But lamplight was bright on the red-and-white tablecloth, and the fire glowed behind the open draughts of the stove.

'We can't sing so soon after eating,' said Pa. 'So I'll just limber up the fiddle.'

Merrily he played, 'Away Down the River on the O-hi-o!' And, 'Why Chime the Bells So Merrily'. And,

> 'Jingle bells, jingle bells,
> Jingle all the way!
> Oh, what fun it is to ride,
> In a one-hoss open sleigh!'

Then he stopped and smiled at them all. 'Are you ready to sing now?'

The voice of the fiddle changed; it was going to sing a hymn. Pa played a few notes. Then they all sang:

> 'Yes, a brighter morn is breaking,
> Better days are coming on.
> All the world will be awaking
> In a new and golden dawn.
> And many nations shall come and say,
> Come, let us go up to the mountains of the Lord!
> And He will teach us, will teach us of His ways,
> And we will walk in His paths.'

The fiddle's voice wandered away, Pa seemed to be playing his thoughts to himself. But a melody grew out of them and throbbed softly until they all joined in and sang:

> 'The sun may warm the grass to life,
> The dew the drooping flower;
> And eyes grow bright and watch the light
> Of autumn's opening hour;
> But words that breathe of tenderness
> And smiles we know are true
> Are warmer than the summertime
> And brighter than the dew.

> 'It is not much the world can give
> With all its subtle art;
> And gold and gems are not the things
> To satisfy the heart;
> But Oh, if those who cluster round
> The altar and the hearth,
> Have gentle words and loving smiles,
> How beautiful the earth!'

Through the music, Mary cried out, 'What's that?'

'What, Mary?' Pa asked.

'I thought I heard – Listen!' Mary said.

They listened. The lamp made a tiny purring sound, and the coals softly settled a little in the stove. Past the little space above the white frost on the windows, falling snow flakes twinkled in the lamplight shining through the glass.

'What did you think you heard, Mary?' Pa asked.

'It sounded like – There it is again!'

This time they all heard a shout. Out in the night, in the storm, a man shouted. And shouted again, quite near the house.

Ma started up. 'Charles! Who on earth?'

CHAPTER 20

THE NIGHT BEFORE CHRISTMAS

PA laid the fiddle in its box, and opened the front door quickly. Snow and cold swirled in, and again a husky shout. 'Hullo-o-o, Ingalls!'

'It's Boast!' Pa cried. 'Come in! Come in!' He snatched his coat and cap, jerked them on and went out into the cold.

'He must be nearly frozen!' Ma exclaimed, and she hurried to put more coal on the fire. From outside came voices and Mr Boast's laugh.

Then the door opened and Pa called, 'Here's Mrs Boast, Caroline. We're going to put up the horses.'

Mrs Boast was a great bundle of coats and blankets. Ma hurried to help her take off layer after layer of wrappings. 'Come to the stove! You must be nearly frozen.'

'Oh, no,' a pleasant voice answered. 'The horse was warm to sit on and Robert wrapped me so tightly in all

140

these blankets, the cold couldn't reach me. He even led the horse so my hands could be under cover.'

'This veil is frozen just the same,' said Ma, unwinding yards of frosted woollen veil from Mrs Boast's head. Mrs Boast's face appeared, framed in a fur-edged hood. Mrs Boast did not look much older than Mary. Her hair was soft brown, and her long-lashed eyes were blue.

'Did you come all this way on horseback, Mrs Boast?' Ma asked her.

'Oh, no. Only about two miles. We were coming in a bobsled, but we got stuck in the snow in a slough. The team and the sled fell down through the snow,' she said. 'Robert got the team out but we had to leave the sled.'

'I know,' said Ma. 'The snow drifts over the top of the tall slough grass, and you can't tell where the slough is. But the grass underneath won't hold up any weight.' She helped Mrs Boast out of her coat.

'Take my chair, Mrs Boast. It's in the warmest place,' Mary urged her. But Mrs Boast said she would sit beside Mary.

Pa and Mr Boast came into the lean-to with a great stamping of snow from their feet. Mr Boast laughed, and in the house everyone laughed, even Ma.

'I don't know why,' Laura said to Mrs Boast. 'We don't even know what the joke is, but when Mr Boast laughs –'

Mrs Boast was laughing too. 'It's contagious,' she said. Laura looked at her blue, laughing eyes and thought that Christmas would be jolly.

Ma was stirring up biscuit. 'How do you do, Mr Boast,' she said. 'You and Mrs Boast must be starved. Supper will be ready in a jiffy.'

Laura put slices of salt pork in the frying˜pan to par-boil, and Ma set the biscuits in the oven. Then Ma drained the pork, dipped the slices in flour and set them to fry, while Laura peeled and sliced potatoes.

'I'll raw-fry them,' Ma said to her low, in the pantry, 'and make milk gravy and a fresh pot of tea. We can make out well enough for food, but what will we do about the presents?'

Laura had not thought of that. They had no presents for Mr and Mrs Boast. Ma whisked out of the pantry to fry the potatoes and make the gravy, and Laura set the table.

'I don't know when I've enjoyed a meal more,' said Mrs Boast, when they had eaten.

'We didn't look for you until spring,' said Pa. 'Winter is a bad time to make such a drive.'

'We found that out,' Mr Boast answered. 'But I tell you, Ingalls, the whole country is moving West in the spring. All Iowa is coming, and we knew we must be ahead of the rush or some claim jumper would be on our homestead. So we came, weather or no weather. You should have filed on a homestead last fall. You'll have to rush it in the spring, or you'll find no land left.'

Pa and Ma looked soberly at each other. They were thinking of the homestead that Pa had found. But Ma only said, 'It's getting late, and Mrs Boast must be tired.'

'I am tired,' Mrs Boast said. 'It was a hard drive, and then to leave the sled and come on horseback through the snowstorm. We were so glad to see your light. And when we came nearer, we heard you singing. You don't know how good it sounded.'

'You take Mrs Boast in with you, Caroline, and Boast and I will bunk down here by the fire,' Pa said. 'We'll have one more song, then all you girls skedaddle.'

He raised the fiddle again from its nest in the box and tried it to see that it was in tune. 'What'll it be, Boast?'

' "Merry Christmas Everywhere",' said Mr Boast. His tenor voice joined Pa's bass. Mrs Boast's soft alto and Laura's soprano and Mary's followed, then Ma's contralto. Carrie's little treble piped up happily.

'Merry, Merry Christmas everywhere!
　　Cheerily it ringeth through the air;
　　Christmas bells, Christmas trees,
　　Christmas odours on the breeze.

'Why should we so joyfully
　　Sing with grateful mirth?
　　See the Sun of Righteousness
　　Beams upon the earth!

'Light for weary wanderers,
　　Comfort for the oppressed;
　　He will guide his trusting ones,
　　Into perfect rest.'

'Good night! Good night!' they all said. Ma came upstairs to get Carrie's bedding for Pa and Mr Boast. 'Their blankets are sopping wet,' she said. 'You three girls can share one bed for one night.'

'Ma! What about the presents?' Laura whispered.

'Never mind, I'll manage somehow,' Ma whispered back. 'Now go to sleep, girls,' she said aloud. 'Good night, sleep tight!'

Downstairs Mrs Boast was softly singing to herself, 'Light for weary wanderers . . .'

CHAPTER 21

MERRY CHRISTMAS

WHEN Laura heard the door shut as Pa and Mr Boast
went out to do the morning chores, she dressed chattering
in the cold and hurried downstairs to help Ma get breakfast.

But Mrs Boast was helping Ma. The room was warm
from the glowing stove. Mush was frying on the long
griddle. The teakettle was boiling and the table was set.

'Merry Christmas!' Ma and Mrs Boast said together.

'Merry Christmas,' Laura answered but she was staring

at the table. At each place, the plate was turned bottom-up over the knife and fork, as usual. But on the plates' bottoms were packages, small packages and larger packages, some wrapped in coloured tissue paper and others in plain wrapping paper tied with coloured string.

'You see, Laura, we didn't hang up stockings last night,' said Ma, 'so we will take our presents off the table at breakfast.'

Laura went back upstairs, and told Mary and Carrie about the Christmas breakfast table. 'Ma knew where we hid all the presents but hers,' she said. 'They are all on the table.'

'But we can't have presents!' Mary wailed horrified. 'There isn't anything for Mr and Mrs Boast!'

'Ma will fix it,' Laura answered. 'She told me so last night.'

'How can she?' Mary asked. 'We didn't know they were coming! There isn't anything we could give them.'

'Ma can fix anything,' said Laura. She took Ma's present from Mary's box and held it behind her when they all went downstairs together. Carrie stood between her and Ma while quickly Laura put the package on Ma's plate. There was a little package on Mrs Boast's plate, and another on Mr Boast's.

'Oh, I can't wait!' Carrie whispered, squeezing her thin hands together. Her peaked face was white and her eyes were big and shining.

'Yes, you can. We've got to,' said Laura. It was easier for Grace, who was so little that she did not notice the Christmas table. But even Grace was so excited that Mary could hardly button her up.

'Mewy Cwismas! Mewy Cwismas!' Grace shouted, wriggling, and when she was free she ran about, shouting, until Ma told her gently that children must be seen and not heard.

'Come here, Grace, and you can see out,' said Carrie. She had blown and wiped a clear space in the frost on the window-pane, and there they stayed, taking turns at looking out, till at last Carrie said, 'Here they come!'

After a loud stamping-off of snow in the lean-to, Pa and Mr Boast came in.

'Merry Christmas! Merry Christmas!' they all cried.

Grace ran behind Ma and clung to her skirts, peeping around them at the strange man. Pa picked her up and tossed her, just as he used to toss Laura when Laura was little. And Grace screamed with laughter just as Laura used to. Laura had to remember hard that she was a big girl now or she would have laughed out loud too. They were all so happy in the warmth full of good smells of cooking, and with company there for Christmas in the snug house. The light from the frost-furred windows was silvery, and just as they all sat down to that exciting Christmas table, the eastern window turned golden; outdoors the stillness of the whole vast snowy prairie was full of sunshine.

'You first, Mrs Boast,' said Ma, for Mrs Boast was company. So Mrs Boast opened her package. In it was a lawn handkerchief edged with narrow crocheted lace. Laura recognized it; it was Ma's best Sunday handkerchief. Mrs Boast was delighted, and so surprised that there was a gift for her.

So was Mr Boast. His present was wristlets, knitted in stripes of red and grey. They fitted him perfectly. They were the wristlets that Ma had knitted for Pa. But she could knit some more for Pa, and the company must have Christmas presents.

Pa said his new socks were exactly what he needed; the cold from the snow had been going right through his boots. And he admired the necktie that Laura had made. 'I'll put this on, right after breakfast!' he said. 'By George, now I'll be all dressed up for Christmas!'

Everyone exclaimed when Ma unwrapped her pretty apron. She put it on at once, and stood up for them all to see. She looked at the hem, and smiled at Carrie. 'You hem very nicely, Carrie,' she said, then she smiled at Laura, 'and Laura's gathers are even, and well sewed. It is a nice apron.'

'There's more, Ma!' Carrie cried out. 'Look in the pocket!'

Ma took out the handkerchief. She was so surprised. And to think that the very morning she gave away her Sunday best handkerchief, she was given another one; it was as if this had been planned, though none of them had planned it. But of course this could not be said in Mrs Boast's hearing. Ma only looked at the handkerchief's tiny hem and said, 'Such a pretty handkerchief too! Thank you, Mary.'

Then everyone admired Mary's bed shoes, and how they had been made of the ends of a worn-out blanket. Mrs Boast said she was going to make some for herself, as soon as any of her blankets wore out.

Carrie put on her mittens and softly clapped her hands. 'My Fourth of July mittens! Oh, see my Fourth of July mittens!' she said.

Then Laura opened her package. And in it was an apron, made of the same calico as Ma's! It was smaller than Ma's apron, and had two pockets. A narrow ruffle was all around it. Ma had cut it out of the other curtain, Carrie had sewed the seams, Mary had hemmed the ruffle. All that time, Ma hadn't known and Laura hadn't known that each was making an apron for the other from those old curtains, and Mary and Carrie had been almost bursting with the two secrets.

'Oh, thank you! Thank you all!' Laura said, smoothing down the pretty white calico with the little red flowers scattered over it. 'Such tiny stitches in the ruffle, Mary! I do thank you.'

Then came the best part of all. Everyone watched while Ma put the little blue coat on Grace and smoothed the swan's-down collar. She put the lovely white swan's-down hood over Grace's golden hair. A bit of the blue silk lining showed around Grace's face and matched her shining eyes. She touched the fluffy soft swan's-down on her wrists, and waved her hands and laughed.

She was so beautiful and so happy, blue and white and gold and alive and laughing, that they could not look at her long enough. But Ma did not want to spoil her with too much attention. So, too soon, she quieted Grace and laid away the coat and hood in the bedroom.

There was still another package beside Laura's plate, and she saw that Mary and Carrie and Grace each had one like it. All at once, they unwrapped them, and each found a little pink cheese-cloth bag full of candy.

'Christmas candy!' Carrie cried and 'Christmas Candy!' Laura and Mary said at the same time.

'However did Christmas candy get here?' Mary asked.

'Why, didn't Santa Claus get here on Christmas Eve?' said Pa. So, almost all at once, they said, 'Oh, Mr Boast! Thank you! Thank you, Mr and Mrs Boast!'

Then Laura gathered up all the paper wrappings, and she helped Ma set on the table the big platter of golden, fried mush, a plate of hot biscuits, a dish of fried potatoes, a bowl of codfish gravy and a glass dish full of dried-apple sauce.

'I'm sorry we have no butter,' said Ma. 'Our cow gives so little milk that we can't make butter any more.'

But the codfish gravy was good on the mush and the potatoes, and nothing could taste better than hot biscuits and applesauce. Such a breakfast as that, like Christmas, came only once a year. And there was still the Christmas dinner to come, on that same day.

After breakfast, Pa and Mr Boast went with the team to

get Mr Boast's bobsled. They took shovels to dig the snow away so that horses could pull it out of the slough.

Then Mary took Grace on her lap in the rocking-chair, and while Carrie made the beds and swept, Ma and Laura and Mrs Boast put on their aprons, rolled up their sleeves and washed the dishes and got dinner.

Mrs Boast was great fun. She was interested in everything, and eager to learn how Ma managed so well.

'When you haven't milk enough to have sour milk, however do you make such delicious biscuits, Laura?' she asked.

'Why, you just use sour dough,' Laura said.

Mrs Boast had never made sour-dough biscuits! It was fun to show her. Laura measured out the cups of sour dough, put in the soda and salt and flour, and rolled out the biscuits on the board.

'But how do you make the sour dough?' Mrs Boast asked.

'You start it,' said Ma, 'by putting some flour and warm water in a jar and letting it stand till it sours.'

'Then when you use it, always leave a little,' said Laura. 'And put in the scraps of biscuit dough, like this, and more warm water,' Laura put in the warm water, 'and cover it,' she put the clean cloth and the plate on the jar, 'and just set it in a warm place,' she set it in its place on the shelf by the stove. 'And it's always ready to use, whenever you want it.'

'I never tasted better biscuits,' said Mrs Boast.

With such good company, the morning seemed to go in a minute. Dinner was almost ready when Pa and Mr Boast came back with the bobsled. The enormous jack rabbit was browning in the oven. Potatoes were boiling, and the coffee pot bubbled on the back of the stove. The house was full of the good smells of roasting meat, hot breads, and coffee. Pa sniffed when he came in.

'Don't worry, Charles,' said Ma. 'You smell coffee, but the kettle is boiling to make your tea.'

'Good! Tea is a man's drink in cold weather,' Pa told her.

Laura spread the clean white tablecloth, and in the centre of the table she set the glass sugar bowl, the glass pitcher full of cream, and the glass spoonholder full of silver spoons all standing on their handles. Around the table Carrie laid the knives and forks, and filled the water glasses, while Laura set all the plates in a pile at Pa's place. Then at each place, all around the table, she cheerfully put a glass sauce dish holding half a canned peach in golden juice. The table was beautiful.

Pa and Mr Boast had washed and combed their hair. Ma put the last empty pot and pan in the pantry, and helped Laura and Mrs Boast whisk the last full dish to the table. Quickly she and Laura took off their work aprons and tied on their Christmas aprons.

'Come!' said Ma. 'Dinner is ready.'

'Come, Boast!' said Pa. 'Sit up and eat hearty! There's plenty more down cellar in a teacup!'

Before Pa, on the big platter, lay the huge roasted rabbit with piles of bread-and-onion stuffing steaming around it. From a dish on one side stood up a mound of mashed potatoes, and on the other side stood a bowl of rich, brown gravy.

There were plates of hot Johnny cake and of small hot biscuits. There was a dish of cucumber pickles.

Ma poured the strong brown coffee and the fragrant tea, while Pa heaped each plate with roast rabbit, stuffing, and potatoes and gravy.

'This is the first time we ever had jack rabbit for Christmas dinner,' Pa said. 'The other time we lived where jack rabbits grow, they were too common, we had them every day. For Christmas we had wild turkey.'

'Yes, Charles, and that was the most we did have,' said Ma. 'There was no surveyors' pantry to get pickles and peaches out of, in Indian Territory.'

'Seems to me this is the best rabbit I ever tasted,' said Mr Boast. 'The gravy is extra good too.'

'Hunger is the best sauce,' Ma replied modestly. But Mrs Boast said, 'I know why the rabbit's so good. Mrs Ingalls lays thin slices of salt pork over it when she roasts it.'

'Why, yes, I do,' Ma agreed. 'I think it does improve the flavour.'

They all took big second helpings. Then Pa and Mr Boast took big third helpings, and Mary and Laura and Carrie did not refuse, but Ma took only a bit of stuffing and Mrs Boast just one more biscuit. 'I declare, I'm so full I can't eat another mouthful,' she said.

When Pa took up the fork from the platter again, Ma warned him. 'Save some room, Charles, you and Mr Boast.'

'You don't mean there's more to come?' said Pa.

Then Ma stepped into the pantry and brought out the dried-apple pie.

'Pie!' said Pa, and, 'Apple pie!' said Mr Boast. 'Jumping Jehoshaphat, I wish I'd known this was coming!'

Slowly they each ate a piece of that apple pie, and Pa and Mr Boast divided the one piece left over.

'I never hope to eat a better Christmas dinner,' said Mr Boast, with a deep sigh of fullness.

'Well,' Pa said. 'It's the first Christmas dinner anybody ever ate in this part of the country. I'm glad it was a good one. In time to come, no doubt a good many folks will celebrate Christmas around here, and I expect they'll have fancier fixings in some ways, but I don't know how they can have more solid comfort than we've got, for a fact.'

After a while he and Mr Boast got up reluctantly, and

Ma began to clear the table. 'I'll do the dishes,' she said to Laura, 'You run help Mrs Boast get settled.'

So Laura and Mrs Boast put on their coats and hoods, mufflers and mittens, and went out into the glittering, biting cold. Laughing, they ploughed and plunged through snow, to the tiny house near by that had been the surveyors' office. At its door Pa and Mr Boast unloaded the bobsled.

The little house had no floor, and it was so small that the double bedstead just fitted across one end. In the corner by the door Pa and Mrs Boast set up the stove. Laura helped Mrs Boast carry the feather bed and quilts and make the bed. Then they set the table against the window opposite the stove, and pushed two chairs under it. Mrs Boast's trunk squeezed between the table and the bed and made another seat. A shelf above the stove and a box beside it held the dishes, and just room enough was left for the door to open against the table.

'There!' Pa said, when all was done. 'Now you folks are settled, come on over. Not even the four of us can get in here, but there's plenty of room at the other house, so that's headquarters. How about a game of checkers, Boast?'

'You go along,' Mrs Boast told them. 'Laura and I will come in a minute.'

When they were gone, Mrs Boast took a full paper bag from under the dishes. 'It's for a surprise,' she told Laura. 'Popcorn! Rob doesn't know I brought it.'

They smuggled the bag into the house and hid it in the pantry, whispering to tell Ma what it was. And later, when Pa and Mr Boast were absorbed in checkers, quietly they heated fat in the iron kettle and poured in a handful of the shelled popcorn. At the first crackle, Pa looked around quickly.

'Popcorn!' he exclaimed. 'I haven't tasted popcorn since

– if I'd known you'd brought popcorn, Boast, I'd have routed it out before now.'

'I didn't bring popcorn,' said Mr Boast. Then he cried out, 'Nell, you rascal!'

'You two go on with your game!' Mrs Boast told him, laughing at him with her blue eyes. 'You're much too busy to notice us.'

'Yes, Charles,' said Ma. 'Don't let us disturb your checkers.'

'I've got you beat anyway, Boast,' said Pa.

'Not yet you haven't,' Mr Boast contradicted.

Ma dipped the snowy kernels from the kettle into a milkpan, and Laura carefully salted them. They popped another kettleful, and the pan would hold no more. Then Mary and Laura and Carrie had a plateful of the crispy crackly melting-soft corn, and Pa and Ma and Mr and Mrs Boast sat around the pan, eating and talking and laughing, till chore-time and supper-time and the time when Pa would play the fiddle.

'Every Christmas is better than the Christmas before,' Laura thought. 'I guess it must be because I'm growing up.'

CHAPTER 22

HAPPY WINTER DAYS

THE Christmasy feeling lasted day after day. Every morning Mrs Boast did her breakfast work quickly and came to spend her time with 'the other girls', as she said. She was always merry and full of fun and always so pretty, with her soft dark hair and laughing blue eyes and the bright colour in her cheeks.

That first week the sun shone brightly, there was no wind, and in six days the snow was all gone. The prairie showed bare and brown, and the air seemed warm as milk. Mrs Boast had cooked the New Year's dinner.

'You can all crowd into my little place for once,' she said.

She let Laura help her move things. They put the table on the bed and opened the door wide against the wall. Then they set the table in the exact middle of the house. One corner of it almost touched the stove, and the other end was almost against the bed. But there was room for them all to come in, single file, and sit around it. Mrs Boast sat by the stove and served the food from its hot top.

First, there was oyster soup. In all her life Laura had never tasted anything so good as that savoury, fragrant, sea-tasting hot milk, with golden dots of melted cream and black specks of pepper on its top, and the little dark canned oysters at its bottom. She sipped slowly, slowly from her spoon, to keep that taste going over her tongue as long as she could.

And with this soup, there were little round oyster crackers. The little oyster crackers were like doll-crackers, and they tasted better because they were so light and small.

When the last drop of soup was gone, and the last crackers divided and crunched, there were hot biscuits with honey, and dried-raspberry sauce. And then a big dishpan full of tender salty popcorn, that had been keeping hot on the back of the stove.

That was the New Year's dinner. It was light but filling. There was something fashionable about it because it was so odd and new, so different, and so daintily served on Mrs Boast's pretty dishes and brand-new tablecloth.

Afterwards they sat talking in the little house, with the soft air coming in and beyond the open door, the brown prairie stretching far away and the soft blue sky curving down to meet it.

'I've never tasted finer honey, Mrs Boast,' said Pa. 'I'm glad you brought it out from Iowa.'

'The oysters too,' said Ma. 'I don't know when I've had such a treat as this dinner.'

'It's a good beginning for 1880,' Pa declared. 'The seventies haven't been so bad, but it looks like the eighties'll be better. If this is a sample of a Dakota winter, we're all lucky we came West.'

'This is certainly a fine country,' Mr Boast agreed. 'I'm glad I've got my claim filed on a hundred and sixty acres of it, and I wish you had, Ingalls.'

'I'll have it before I'm a week older,' said Pa. 'I've been waiting for the land office to open at Brookins, to save me more than a week's travel to Yankton and back. They said the Brookins office would open the first of the year, and by Jove, with weather like this I'm starting tomorrow! If Caroline says so.'

'I do, Charles,' Ma said quietly. Her eyes, her whole face, were shining with gladness because now, so soon, Pa would surely have their homestead.

'That settles it,' said Pa. 'Not that I figure there's any danger of being too late, but it might as well be done and over with.'

'The sooner the better, Ingalls,' Mr Boast said. 'I tell you, you've got no notion what the rush is going to be this spring.'

'Well, nobody'll be there quicker than I'll be,' Pa answered. 'Starting before sun-up, I ought to show up at the land office bright and early day after tomorrow morning. So if you folks want to send any letters back to Iowa, get 'em fixed up and I'll take 'em along and mail them in Brookins.'

That ended New Year's dinner. Mrs Boast and Ma were writing letters that afternoon, and Ma packed a lunch for Pa to take with him. But at nightfall a wind full of snow was blowing and frost began to creep up the window-panes again.

'This is no kind of weather to go anywhere,' Pa said. 'Don't worry about the homestead, Caroline. I'll get it.'

'Yes, Charles, I know you will,' Ma replied.

In the stormy weather Pa tended his trap lines and stretched skins to dry. Mr Boast hauled brushwood from Lake Henry and chopped it up to burn, for he had no coal. And every day Mrs Boast came.

Often when the sun was shining, she and Laura and Carrie, well wrapped-up, played in the deep snow together. They wrestled and ran and threw snowballs, and one day they made a snowman. And hand in hand in the sharp, bright cold the three of them ran and slid on the ice of Silver Lake. Laura had never laughed so much.

Late one afternoon, when they had been sliding and were coming home warm and breathless, Mrs Boast said, 'Laura, come over to my house a minute.'

Laura went with her and Mrs Boast showed her a tall stack of newspapers. She had brought all those New York Ledgers from Iowa.

'Take as many as you can carry,' she said. 'When you get them read, bring them back and get some more.'

Laura ran all the way home with an armful of papers. She burst into the house and dropped them in Mary's lap.

'See, Mary! See what I've brought!' she cried. 'Stories! They're all stories!'

'Oh, hurry up and get the supper work done so we can read,' Mary said eagerly. But Ma said, 'Never mind the work, Laura! Read us a story!'

So while Ma and Carrie got supper, Laura began to read to them all a wonderful story, about dwarfs and caves where robbers lived and a beautiful lady who was lost in the caves. At the most exciting part she came suddenly to the words, 'To be continued.' And there was not another word of that story.

'Oh, dear me, we never will know what became of that lady,' Mary lamented. 'Laura, why do you suppose they print only part of a story?'

'Why do they, Ma?' Laura asked.

'They don't,' said Ma. 'Look at the next paper.'

Laura looked, at the next and the next and next. 'Oh, here it is!' she cried. 'And more – and more – It goes right on down through the pile. It's all here, Mary! Here it says, "The End".'

'It's a continued story,' said Ma. Laura and Mary had never before heard of a continued story, but Ma had.

'Well,' Mary said contentedly. 'Now we can save the next part for tomorrow. Every day we can read one part, and that will make the stories last longer.'

'That's my wise girls,' said Ma. So Laura did not say that she would rather read as fast as she could. She laid the papers carefully away. Every day she read one more part of the story, and then they wondered until next day what would happen next to the beautiful lady.

On the stormy days, Mrs Boast brought her sewing or knitting, and those were cosy days of reading and talking. One day Mrs Boast told them about whatnots. She said that everyone in Iowa was making whatnots, and she would show them how.

So she told Pa how to make the shelves, three-cornered, to fit in a corner. He made five shelves of graduated sizes, the largest at the bottom and the smallest at the top, all fastened solidly with narrow strips of board between them. When he had finished, the whatnot fitted snugly into a corner of the room and stood firmly on three legs. Its top shelf was as high as Ma could easily reach.

Then Mrs Boast cut a curtain of pasteboard to hang from the edge of each shelf. She scalloped the bottom of the pasteboard, a large scallop in the middle and a smaller scallop at each side. The pieces of pasteboard and the scallops were graduated like the shelves, from large at the bottom to small at the top.

Next Mrs Boast showed them how to cut and fold small squares of heavy wrapping paper. They folded each square cornerwise and then across, and pressed it smooth. When dozens of the squares were folded, Mrs Boast showed Laura how to sew them in rows on the pasteboard, close together, with points down. Each row overlapped the row below it, and each point must lie between two points of the row below it, and the rows must follow the scallops' curves.

While they worked in the snug, cosy house, they told stories and sang and talked. Ma and Mrs Boast talked mostly about the homesteads. Mrs Boast had seeds enough for two gardens; she said she would divide with Ma, so Ma need not worry about seeds. When the town was built, there might be seeds in town to sell, but again there might not. So Mrs Boast had brought plenty from the gardens of her friends in Iowa.

'I'll be thankful when we've settled,' Ma said. 'This is the last move we're going to make. Mr Ingalls agreed to that before we left Minnesota. My girls are going to have schooling and lead a civilized life.'

Laura did not know whether or not she wanted to be settled down. When she had schooling, she would have to teach school, and she would rather think of something else. She would rather sing than think at all. She could hum very softly without interrupting the talk, and then often Ma and Mrs Boast and Mary and Carrie would sing with her. Mrs Boast had taught them two new songs. Laura liked 'The Gypsy's Warning'.

> 'Do not trust him, gentle lady,
> Though his voice be low and sweet,
> Heed not him who kneels before you,
> Gently pleading at your feet,

> Now thy life is in the morning,
> Cloud not this, thy happy lot,
> Listen to the gypsy's warning,
> Gentle lady, heed him not.'

The other new song was, 'When I Was One and Twenty, Nell, and You Were Seventeen'. It was Mr Boast's favourite song. He had been twenty-one when he met Mrs Boast, and she had been seventeen. Her name was really Ella, but Mr Boast called her Nell.

At last the five pasteboard pieces were neatly covered with rows above rows of the little paper points, and no stitches showed except along the top of the top row. Then Mrs Boast sewed a wide strip of the brown paper above these stitches and folded it over to hide them.

Finally, they tacked each pasteboard curtain to its shelf. The stiff scallops, covered with the stiff little paper points, hung down stiffly. Then Pa carefully painted the whole whatnot, and all the little paper points, a rich, dark brown. When the paint dried, they set the whatnot in the corner behind Mary's chair.

'So that's a whatnot,' Pa said.

'Yes,' said Ma. 'Isn't it pretty?'

'It's a neat job,' said Pa.

'Mrs Boast says they're all the rage in Iowa,' she told him.

'Well, she ought to know,' Pa agreed. 'And there's nothing in Iowa too good for you, Caroline.'

But the best time of all was after supper. Every evening Pa played the fiddle, and now Mr Boast's and Mrs Boast's beautiful voices rounded out the singing. Gaily Pa played and sang:

> 'When I was young and single,
> I could make the money jingle
> And the world went well with me then, O then!
> The world went well with me then.

'I married me a wife, O then! O then!
I married me a wife, O then!
I married me a wife, she was the joy of my life,
And the world went well with me then!'

The song went on to say that she was not such a good
wife after all, so Pa never sang the rest of it. His eyes
twinkled at Ma while the music laughed and whirled and
then he would sing:

'She can make a cherry pie,
Billy boy! Billy boy!
She can make a cherry pie,
Charming Billy.
She can make a cherry pie
With a twinkle in her eye
But she's a young thing
And cannot leave her mother.'

The music would go rollicking while only Pa and Mr
Boast sang:

'I bet my money on the bob-tailed mare
And you bet yours on the grey!'

Even in songs Ma did not approve of gambling, but
her toe could not stop tapping while Pa played such
tunes.

Then every evening they all sang one round. Mr Boast's
tenor would begin, 'Three blind mice,' and go on while
Mrs Boast's alto began, 'Three blind mice,' then as she
went on Pa's bass would join in, 'Three blind mice,' and
then Laura's soprano, and Ma's contralto, and Mary
and Carrie. When Mr Boast reached the end of the song he
began it again without stopping, and they all followed, each
behind the other, going round and round with words and
music.

'Three blind mice! Three blind mice!
They all ran after the farmer's wife
She cut off their tails with a carving knife,
Did you ever hear such a tale in your life
Of three blind mice?'

They kept on singing until someone laughed and then the song ended ragged and breathless and laughing. And Pa would play some of the old songs, 'to go to sleep on', he said.

'Nellie was a lady, last night she died,
Oh, toll the bell for lovely Nell,
My old–Vir-gin-ia bride.'

And,

'Oh, do you remember sweet Alice, Ben Bolt?
Sweet Alice with eyes so brown,
Who wept with delight when you gave her a smile,
And trembled with fear at your frown?'

And,

'Oft in the stilly night,
Ere slumber's chain has bound me,
Sweet memory brings the light
Of other days around me.'

Laura had never been so happy, and for some reason she was happiest of all when they were singing,

'Ye banks and braes of Bonny Doon,
How can ye bloom sae fresh and fair?
How can ye chaunt, ye little birds,
And I sae weary, full of care?'

CHAPTER 23

ON THE PILGRIM WAY

ONE Sunday evening Pa's fiddle was singing a Sunday tune and they were all singing heartily with it,

> 'When cheerful we meet in our pleasant home
> And the song of joy is swelling,
> Do we pause to think of the tears that flow
> In sorrow's lonely dwelling?
> Let us lend a hand –'

The fiddle stopped suddenly. Outdoors a strong voice was singing:

> '– to those who are faint and weary.
> Let us lend a hand to those on the pilgrim way.'

The fiddle squawked in amazement as Pa dropped it on the table and hurried to the door. The cold burst in and the door slammed behind him. Outside it there was an outburst of voices; then the door flung open and two snowy men stumbled in while Pa said behind them, 'I'll see to putting up your team, be with you right away.'

One of the men was tall and thin. Between his cap and muffler Laura saw blue, kind eyes. Before she knew what she was doing she heard herself screaming, 'Reverend Alden! Reverend Alden!'

'Not Brother Alden!' Ma exclaimed. 'Why, Brother Alden!'

He had taken off his cap and now they could all see his pleasant eyes and his dark brown hair.

'We are pleased to see you, Brother Alden,' Ma said. 'Come to the fire. This is a surprise!'

'You are no more surprised than I am, Sister Ingalls,' said the Reverend Alden. 'I left you folks settled on Plum Creek. I had no idea you were 'way out West. And here are my little country girls grown into women!'

Laura could not say a word. Her throat was choked with the joy of seeing Reverend Alden again. But Mary said politely, 'We are glad to see you again, sir.' Mary's face was shining with gladness; only her sightless eyes were blank. They startled Reverend Alden. He looked quickly at Ma, and then at Mary again.

'Mr and Mrs Boast, our neighbours, Reverend Alden,' said Ma.

Reverend Alden said, 'You were all doing some fine singing when we drove up,' and Mr Boast said, 'You did some fine singing yourself, sir.'

'Oh, I wasn't the one who joined in,' said Reverend Alden. 'That was Scotty, here. I was too cold, but his red hair keeps him warm. Reverend Stuart, these are old, good friends of mine, and their friends, so we are all friends together.'

Reverend Stuart was so young that he was not much

more than a big boy. His hair was flaming red, his face was red with cold, and his eyes were a sparkling cold grey.

'Set the table, Laura,' Ma said quietly, tying on her apron. Mrs Boast put on an apron too, and they were all busy, poking up the fire, setting the kettle to boil for tea, making biscuits, frying potatoes, while Mr Boast talked to the visitors who stood in the way, thawing themselves by the stove. Pa came from the stable with two more men, who owned the team. They were homesteaders, going out to settle on the Jim River.

Laura heard Reverend Alden say, 'We two are just passengers. We hear there's a settlement on the Jim, a town named Huron. The Home Missionary Society sent us out to look over the ground and make ready to start a church there.'

'I guess there's a town-site marked out on the railroad grade,' said Pa. 'But I never heard of any building there, except a saloon.'

'All the more reason we should get a church started,' Reverend Alden answered cheerfully.

After the travellers had eaten supper, he came to the door of the pantry where Ma and Laura were washing the dishes. He thanked Ma for the good supper and then he said, 'I am sorry indeed, Sister Ingalls, to see the affliction that has come to Mary.'

'Yes, Brother Alden,' Ma answered sadly. 'Sometimes it is hard to be resigned to God's will. We all had scarlet fever in our place on Plum Creek, and for a while it was hard to get along. But I'm thankful that all the children were spared to us. Mary is a great comfort to me, Brother Alden. She has never once repined.'

'Mary is a rare soul, and a lesson to all of us,' said Reverend Alden. 'We must remember that whom the Lord loveth, He chasteneth, and a brave spirit will turn all our afflictions to good. I don't know whether you and Brother

Ingalls know that there are colleges for the blind. There is one in Iowa.'

Ma took tight hold of the edge of the dishpan. Her face startled Laura. Her gentle voice sounded choked and hungry. She asked, 'How much does it cost?'

'I don't know, Sister Ingalls,' Reverend Alden answered. 'I will make inquiries for you if you like.'

Ma swallowed and went on washing dishes. She said, 'We can't afford it. But perhaps, later – if it doesn't cost too much, we might somehow manage, sometime. I always wanted Mary to have an education.'

Laura's heart beat hard and thick. She could feel its beating in her throat, and wild thoughts fluttered so fast in her mind that she did not know what any of them were.

'We must trust in the Lord to do all things for our best good,' said Reverend Alden. 'Shall we have a short prayer meeting, all of us together, when you've finished the dishes?'

'Yes, Brother Alden, I should like that,' said Ma. 'I am sure we all would.'

When the dishes were done and their hands washed, Ma and Laura took off their aprons and smoothed their hair. Reverend Alden and Mary were talking together earnestly while Mrs Boast held Grace, and Mr Boast and the two homesteaders were talking to Reverend Stuart and Pa about the wheat and oats he intended to raise as soon as he could get his sod broken. When Ma came in, Reverend Alden stood up and said they would all have the refreshment of prayer together before saying good night.

They all knelt down by their chairs, and Reverend Alden asked God, who knew their hearts and their secret thoughts, to look down on them there, and to forgive their sins and help them to do right. A quietness was in the room while he spoke. Laura felt as if she were hot, dry, dusty grass parching in a drought, and the quietness was a cool and gentle rain falling on her. It truly was a refreshment. Everything was simple now that she felt so cool and strong, and she would be glad to work hard and go without anything she wanted herself, so that Mary could go to college.

Then Mr and Mrs Boast thanked Brother Alden and went home, and Laura and Carrie brought Carrie's bed downstairs. Ma made it down on the floor by the stove.

'We've only the one bed,' Ma apologized, 'and I'm afraid there are not covers enough for it.'

'Don't worry, Sister Ingalls,' said Reverend Alden. 'We'll use our overcoats.'

'We'll be very comfortable, I'm sure,' said Reverend Stuart. 'And glad we are to have found you folks here. We thought we had to go all the way to Huron, until we saw your light and heard you singing.'

Upstairs, Laura helped Carrie unbutton in the dark. She tucked the hot flat-iron close against Mary's feet in the bed. As they all snuggled tight together to get warm under the icy-cold covers, they heard Pa and the travellers still talking and laughing around the fire.

'Laura,' Mary whispered, 'Reverend Alden told me there are colleges for blind people.'

'What, for blind people?' Carrie whispered.

'Colleges,' whispered Laura, 'where they get college educations.'

'How can they?' Carrie asked. 'I thought you had to read, to study.'

'I don't know,' Mary said. 'Anyway, I couldn't go. It must cost something. I don't suppose there's any chance I could.'

'Ma knows,' Laura whispered. 'Reverend Alden told her too. Maybe you can, Mary. I do hope you can.' She took a deep breath and promised, 'I will study hard, so I can teach school and help.'

In the morning the travellers' voices and a clatter of

dishes woke her and she sprang out of bed to dress and hurry downstairs to help Ma.

Outdoors was crisp and cold. Sunshine gilded the frosty windows, and in the house everyone was hearty and cheerful. How the travellers did enjoy that breakfast! They praised everything they ate. The biscuits were light and flaky, the fried potatoes were brown and finely hashed, the slices of fat pork were thin and crisp, and the gravy was smooth and brown and creamy. There was hot brown-sugar syrup, and plenty of fragrant steaming tea.

'This meat is delicious,' Reverend Stuart said. 'I know it is just fat salt pork, but I never tasted any like it. Would you tell me how you cook it, Sister Ingalls?'

Ma was surprised, and Reverend Alden explained, 'Scotty's going to stay out here in this missionary field. I've only come out to get him started. He'll be baching and doing his own cooking.'

'Do you know how to cook, Brother Stuart?' Ma asked, and he said he expected to learn by experience. He had brought supplies; beans, flour, salt, tea and salt pork.

'The meat is easy,' said Ma. 'Cut the slices thin, and set them to parboil in cold water. When the water boils, pour it off. Then roll the slices in flour and fry them brown. When they are crisp, take them out on to a platter, and pour some of the fat off. Save it to use for butter. Then brown some flour in the fat left in the frying pan, pour in some milk, and keep stirring it as it boils until the gravy is just right.'

'Would you mind writing it down?' said Reverend Stuart. 'How much flour, and how much milk?'

'Goodness!' said Ma. 'I never measure, but I guess I can make a stab at it.' She got a sheet of paper and her little pearl-handled pen and the ink bottle, and wrote down her receipts for fried salt pork and gravy, and for sourdough biscuits and bean soup and baked beans, while

Laura cleared the table quickly and Carrie ran to ask Mr and Mrs Boast to come over for a preaching service.

It seemed odd to have church on Monday morning, but the travellers were starting on the last stage of their journey to Huron, and no one wanted to lose this opportunity to hear a sermon.

Pa played the fiddle, and they all sang a hymn. Reverend Stuart, with Ma's receipts in his pocket, made a short prayer for guidance in all their worthy endeavours. Then Reverend Alden preached the sermon. After that, Pa's fiddle gaily and sweetly played and they all sang:

'There is a happy land, far, far away,
  Where saints in glory stand, bright, bright as day,
  Oh, to hear the angels sing glory to the Lord, our King . . .'

When the team and wagon were ready to start, Reverend Alden said, 'You have had the first church service in this new town. In the spring I will be back to organize a church.' And he said to Mary and Laura and Carrie, 'We will have a Sunday school too! You can all help with a Christmas Tree next Christmas.'

He climbed into the wagon and went away, leaving them with that to think about and look forward to. Wrapped in shawls and coats and mufflers, they stood watching the wagon going westward on the untouched snow and leaving the marks of its wheels behind it. The cold sun shone brightly and the white world glittered millions of tiny, sharp points of light.

'Well,' Mrs Boast said through a fold of shawl drawn across her mouth, 'it's nice to have had the first church service here.'

'What is the name of the town that's going to be here?' Carries asked.

'It doesn't have a name yet, does it, Pa?' said Laura.

'Yes,' Pa answered. 'It's De Smet. It's named for a

French priest who came pioneering out here in the early days.'

They went into the warm house. 'That poor boy'll ruin his health, most likely,' said Ma. 'Baching all by himself and trying to live on his own cooking.' She meant Reverend Stuart.

'He's Scotch,' said Pa, as if that meant that he would be all right.

'What did I tell you, Ingalls, about the spring rush?' said Mr Boast. 'Two homesteaders in here already, and March hardly begun.'

'That struck me too,' said Pa. 'I'm making tracks for Brookins tomorrow morning, rain or shine.'

CHAPTER 24

THE SPRING RUSH

'No music tonight,' Pa said that evening at the supper table. 'Early to bed and early to rise, and day after tomorrow our claim's filed on the homestead.'

'I'll be glad, Charles,' said Ma. After all the bustle of last night and this morning, the house was quiet and composed again. The supper work was done, Grace slept in the trundle bed, and Ma was packing the lunch that Pa would eat on the way to Brookins.

'Listen,' Mary said. 'I hear somebody talking.'

Laura pressed her face to a window-pane and shut out the lamplight with her hands. Against the snow she saw a dark team and a wagon full of men. One of them shouted again, then another jumped to the ground. Pa went to meet him and they stood talking. Then Pa came in and shut the door behind him.

'There's five of them, Caroline,' he said. 'Strangers, on their way to Huron.'

'There isn't room for them here,' said Ma.

'Caroline, we've got to put them up for the night. There isn't any other place they can stay or get a bite to eat. Their team is tired out and they're greenhorns. If they try to get to Huron tonight, they'll lose themselves on the prairie and maybe freeze to death.'

Ma sighed. 'Well, you know best, Charles.'

So Ma cooked supper for the five strange men. They filled the place with their loud boots and loud voices, and their bedding piled in heaps, ready to make their beds on the floor by the stove. Even before the supper dishes were finished, Ma took her hands from the dishwater and said quietly, 'It's bed-time, girls.'

It was not bed-time, but they knew that she meant they were not allowed to stay downstairs among those strange men. Carrie followed Mary through the stair door, but Ma held Laura back to slip into her hand a strong sliver of wood. 'Push this into the slot above the latch,' Ma said. 'Push it in well and leave it there. Then no one can lift the latch and open the door. I want the door to be locked. Don't come down till I call you tomorrow morning.'

In the morning, Laura and Mary and Carrie lay in bed after the sun was up. Downstairs they heard the strangers talking, and breakfast dishes clattering.

'Ma said not to come till she called us,' Laura insisted.

'I wish they'd go away,' said Carrie. 'I don't like strangers.'

'I don't either, and neither does Ma,' Laura said. 'It takes them a long time to get started, because they're green-horns.'

At last they were gone, and at dinner Pa said he would go to Brookins tomorrow. 'No use starting unless I start early,' he said. 'It's a long day's trip, and there's no sense in starting after sun-up and having to camp out overnight in this cold.'

That night more strangers came. The next night there were more. Ma said, 'Mercy on us, aren't we to have one night in peace by ourselves?'

'I can't help it, Caroline,' said Pa. 'We can't refuse folks shelter, when there's nowhere else they can stay.'

'We can charge them for it, Charles,' Ma said firmly. Pa did not like to charge folks for shelter and a meal, but he knew that Ma was right. So he charged twenty-five cents a meal, and twenty-five cents for shelter overnight, for man or horse.

There was no more singing, no more comfortable suppers or cosy evenings. Every day more strangers crowded around the supper table and every night as soon as all the dishes were washed, Laura and Mary and Carrie had to go up to the attic and fasten the door behind them.

The strangers came from Iowa, from Ohio, from Illinois and Michigan, from Wisconsin and Minnesota and even from far-away New York and Vermont. They were going to Huron or to Fort Pierre or even farther West, looking for homesteads.

One morning Laura sat up in bed, listening. 'Where's Pa, I wonder?' she said. 'I don't hear Pa's voice. That's Mr Boast talking.'

'Maybe he's gone to get the homestead,' Mary guessed.

When at last the loaded wagons went away to the West and Ma called the girls downstairs, she said that Pa had started before sun-up. 'He didn't want to go and leave us in this rush,' she said, 'but he had to. Someone else will get the homestead if he doesn't hurry. We had no idea that people would rush in here like this, and March hardly begun.'

This was the first week in March. The door was open, and the air felt like spring.

'When March comes in like a lamb, it goes out like a lion,' said Ma. 'Come, girls, there's work to be done. Let's get this house in order before more travellers come.'

'I wish nobody'd come till Pa gets back,' Laura said while she and Carrie washed the stacks of dishes.

'Maybe nobody will,' Carrie hoped.

'Mr Boast is going to look after things while your Pa's gone,' Ma said. 'He asked Mr and Mrs Boast to stay here. They'll sleep in the bedroom, and Grace and I'll go upstairs with you girls.'

Mrs Boast came to help. That day they cleaned the whole house and moved the beds. They were all very tired, when in the last of the sunset they saw a wagon coming from the East. There were five men in it.

Mr Boast helped them put their horses in the stable. Mrs Boast helped Ma cook their suppers. They had not finished eating, when another wagon brought four men. Laura cleared the table, washed the dishes, and helped put supper on the table for them. While they were eating, a third wagon brought six men.

Mary had gone upstairs to be away from the crowd. Carrie sang Grace to sleep in the bedroom with the door shut. Laura cleared the table again and washed the dishes again.

'This is the worst yet,' Ma said to Mrs Boast when they met in the pantry. 'There isn't room for fifteen on the floor, we'll have to put some beds in the lean-to. And they'll have to use their robes and blankets and coats for bedding.'

'Rob will tend to it, I'll speak to him,' said Mrs Boast. 'Mercy me, that's not another wagon?'

Laura had to wash the dishes again and reset the table again. The house was so full of strange men, strange eyes and strange voices and bulky coats and muddy boots, that she could hardly get through the crowd.

At last they were all fed, and for the last time the last

dish was washed. Ma with Grace in her arms followed Laura and Carrie to the stairs, and carefully fastened the door behind them. Mary was sleeping in bed, and Laura could not keep her eyes open while she undressed. But as soon as she lay down, she was awakened by the noise downstairs.

There was loud talking and walking. Ma sat up to listen. The downstairs bedroom was still, so Mr Boast must think that the noise was all right. Ma lay down again. The noise grew louder. Sometimes it almost stopped, then suddenly it burst out. A crash shook the house, and Laura sat straight up, crying out, 'Ma! What's that?'

Ma's voice was so low that it seemed louder than all the shouting downstairs. 'Be quiet, Laura,' she said. 'Lie down.'

Laura thought she could not sleep. She was so tired that the noise tormented her. But another crash woke her out of a sound sleep. Ma said, 'It's all right, Laura. Mr Boast is there.' Laura slept again.

In the morning Ma gently shook her awake, and whispered, 'Come Laura, it's time to get breakfast. Let the others sleep.'

They went downstairs together. Mr Boast had taken up the beds. Tousled, sleepy and red-eyed, the men were getting into their boots and coats. Ma and Mrs Boast hurried breakfast. The table was small, there were not dishes enough, so that Laura set the table and washed the dishes three times.

At last the men were gone, and Ma called Mary, while she and Mrs Boast cooked more breakfast and Laura washed dishes and set the table once more.

'My, such a night!'

'What was the matter?' Mary wondered.

'I think they were drunk,' Ma said, tight-lipped.

'I should say they were!' Mr Boast told her. 'They

brought bottles and a jug of whisky. I thought once I would have to interfere, but what could I do against a crowd of fifteen drunks? I decided to let them fight it out, unless they set the house afire.'

'I'm thankful they didn't,' said Ma.

That day a young man drove up to the house with a load of lumber. He had hauled the boards from Brookins, to build a store on the town-site. Pleasantly he urged Ma to board him while he was building, and Ma could not refuse because there was no other place where he could eat.

Next came a man and his son from Sioux Falls. They had brought lumber to build a grocery store. They begged Ma to board them, and after she had agreed she said to Laura, 'Might as well be hung for a sheep as a lamb.'

'If Ingalls doesn't hurry back, we'll have a town here before he comes,' said Mr Boast.

'I only hope he's not too late to file on the homestead,' Ma replied anxiously.

CHAPTER 25

PA'S BET

THAT day did not seem real. Laura's eyelids felt sandy and she yawned all the time, yet she did not feel sleepy. At noon young Mr Hinz and the two Mr Harthorns came to dinner. In the afternoon their hammers could be heard pounding on the framework of the new buildings. It seemed a long time since Pa had gone.

He did not come that night. All the next day he did not

come. That night he did not come. And now Laura was sure that he was having a hard time to get the homestead. Perhaps he might not get it. If he did not get it, perhaps they would go west to Oregon.

Ma would not let any more strangers sleep in the house. Only Mr Hinz and the two Harthorns bunked down on the floor by the stove. The weather was not so cold that men would freeze, sleeping in their wagons. Ma charged twenty-five cents just for supper, and far into the night she and Mrs Boast cooked and Laura washed dishes. So many men came to eat that she did not try to count them.

Late in the afternoon of the fourth day Pa came home. He waved as he drove by to put the tired team in the stable, and he walked smiling into the house. 'Well, Caroline! Girls!' he said. 'We've got the claim.'

'You got it!' Ma exclaimed joyfully.

'I went after it, didn't I?' Pa laughed. 'Brrr! It's chilly, riding. Let me get to the stove and warm myself.'

Ma shook down the fire and set the kettle boiling for tea. 'Did you have any trouble, Charles?' she asked.

'You wouldn't believe it,' said Pa. 'I never saw such a jam. It looks like the whole country's trying to file on land. I got to Brookins all right the first night, and next morning when I showed up at the Land Office I couldn't get anywheres near the door. Every man had to stand in line and wait his turn. So many were ahead of me that my turn didn't come that day.'

'You didn't stand there all day, Pa?' Laura cried.

'Yep, Flutterbudget. All day.'

'Without anything to eat? Oh, no, Pa!' said Carrie.

'Pshaw, that didn't worry me. What worried me was the crowds. I kept thinking maybe somebody ahead of me is getting my quarter section. Caroline, you never saw such crowds. But my worry then wasn't a patch to what came later.'

'What, Pa?' Laura asked.

'Let a fellow get his breath, Flutterbudget! Well, when the Land Office closed I went along in the jam to get supper at the hotel, and I heard a couple of men talking. One had filed on a claim near Huron. The other said De Smet was going to be a better town than Huron, and then he mentioned the very piece I picked out last winter. He told the numbers. He was going to file on it first thing next morning. He said it was the only piece left vacant anywhere near this town-site. So he was going to have it, though he'd never seen it.

'Well, that was enough for me. I had to beat him to that claim. At first I thought I'd be up bright and early next morning, and then I figured I wouldn't take any chances. So as soon as I got some supper, I made tracks for the Land Office.'

'I thought it was closed,' said Carrie.

'It was. I settled right down on the doorstep to spend the night.'

'Surely you didn't need to do that, Charles?' said Ma, handing him a cup of tea.

'Need to do that?' Pa repeated. 'I wasn't the only man who had that idea, not by a blamed sight. Lucky I got there first. Must have been forty men waiting there all night, and right next to me were those two fellows that I'd heard talking.'

He blew on the tea to cool it, and Laura said, 'But they didn't know you wanted that piece, did they?'

'They didn't know me from Adam,' said Pa, drinking the tea, 'till a fellow came along and sang out, "Hullo, Ingalls! So you weathered the winter on Silver Lake. Settling down at De Smet, uh?"'

'Oh, Pa!' Mary wailed.

'Yes, the fat was in the fire then,' said Pa. 'I knew I wouldn't have a chance if I budged from that door. So

I didn't. By sun-up the crowd was doubled, and a couple of hundred men must have been pushing and shoving against me before the Land Office opened. There wasn't any standing in line that day, I tell you! It was each fellow for himself and devil take the hindmost.

'Well, girls, finally the door opened. How about some more tea, Caroline?'

'Oh, Pa, go *on*!' Laura cried. 'Please.'

'Just as it opened,' said Pa, 'the Huron man crowded me back. "Get in! I'll hold him!" he said to the other fellow. It meant a fight, and while I fought him, the other'd get my homestead. Right then, quick as a wink, somebody landed like a ton of brick on the Huron man. "Go in, Ingalls!" he yelled. "I'll fix 'im! Yow-ee-ee!"'

Pa's long, catamount screech curled against the walls, and Ma gasped, 'Mercy! Charles!'

'And you'll never guess who it was,' said Pa.

'Mr Edwards!' Laura shouted.

Pa was astounded. 'How did you guess it, Laura?'

'He yelled like that in Indian Territory. He's a wildcat from Tennessee,' Laura remembered. 'Oh, Pa, where is he? Did you bring him?'

'I couldn't get him to come home with me,' said Pa. 'I tried every persuasion I could think of, but he's filed on a claim south of here and must stay with it to keep off claim jumpers. He told me to remember him to you, Caroline, and to Mary and Laura. I'd never have got the claim if it hadn't been for him. Golly, that was a fight he started!'

'Was he hurt?' Mary asked anxiously.

'Not a scratch. He just started that fight. He got out of it as quick as I ducked inside and started filing my claim. But it was some time before the crowd quieted down. They –'

'All's well that ends well, Charles,' Ma interrupted.

'I guess so, Caroline,' Pa said. 'Yes, I guess that's right. Well, girls, I've bet Uncle Sam fourteen dollars against a hundred and sixty acres of land, that we can make out to live on the claim for five years. Going to help me win the bet?'

'Oh, yes, Pa!' Carrie said eagerly, and Mary said, 'Yes, Pa!' gladly, and Laura promised soberly, 'Yes, Pa.'

'I don't like to think of it as gambling,' Ma said in her gentle way.

'Everything's more or less a gamble, Caroline,' said Pa. 'Nothing is certain but death and taxes.'

CHAPTER 26

THE BUILDING BOOM

THERE was no time for a good, long talk with Pa. Already
the sunshine from the western window slanted far across the
floor, and Ma said, 'We must be getting supper. The men
will be here soon.'

'What men?' Pa asked.

'Oh, wait, Ma, please, I want to show him,' Laura
begged. 'It's a surprise, Pa!' She hurried into the pantry,
and from the almost empty sack of beans where it was hidden, she pulled out the little sack full of money. 'Look, Pa,
look!'

Pa felt the little sack in amazement. He looked at their

faces, all shining with smiles. 'Caroline! What have you girls been up to?'

'Look inside, Pa!' Laura cried. She could not wait while he untied the little sack. 'Fifteen dollars and twenty-five cents!'

'I'll be jiggered!' Pa said.

Then while Laura and Ma started to get supper, they told him all that had happened while he was away. Before they had finished talking, another wagon pulled up at the door. There were seven strangers at supper that night; another dollar and seventy-five cents. And now that Pa was at home, the strangers could sleep on the floor around the stove. Laura did not care how many dishes she washed, nor how sleepy and tired she was. Pa and Ma were getting rich, and she was helping.

In the morning she was surprised. There was hardly time to talk; so many men were there for breakfast, she could hardly wash the dishes fast enough, and when at last she could empty the dishpan and hang it up there was hardly time to sweep and scrub the muddy floor before she must begin peeling potatoes for dinner. She had only a glimpse of the sunny, cold, blue-and-white-and-brown March day outdoors, while she emptied the dishpan. And she saw Pa driving a load of lumber towards the town-site.

'What on earth is Pa doing?' she asked Ma.

'He's putting up a building on the town-site,' said Ma.

'Who for?' Laura asked, beginning to sweep. Her fingers were shrunken in ridges, from being so long in the dishwater.

'"For whom", Laura,' Ma corrected her. 'For himself,' and she tugged through the doorway an armful of bedding that she was taking outdoors to air.

'I thought we were going to move to the claim,' Laura said when Ma came in.

'We have six months before we must build on the

homestead,' said Ma. 'Lots in town are going so fast your Pa thinks he can make money by building on one. He's using the lumber from the railroad shanties and putting up a store building to sell.'

'Oh, Ma, isn't it wonderful, all the money we're making!' Laura said, sweeping vigorously while Ma gathered another armful of bedding.

'Draw the broom, Laura; don't flip it, that raises the dust,' said Ma. 'Yes, but we mustn't count chickens before they're hatched.'

That week the house filled with steady boarders, men who were building houses on the town-site or on their homestead claims. From dawn until far into the night, Ma and Laura hardly had time to catch their breaths. All day long there was a racket of wagons passing. Teamsters were hauling lumber from Brookins as fast as they could, and yellow skeletons of buildings rose every day. Already you could see Main Street growing up from the muddy ground along the railroad grade.

Every night beds covered the floor of the big room and the lean-to. Pa slept on the floor with the boarders so that Mary and Laura and Carrie could move into the bedroom with Ma and Grace, and more boarders' beds covered the whole floor of the attic.

The supplies were all gone, and now Ma had to buy flour and salt and beans and meat and corn meal, so she did not make so much money. Supplies cost three and four times as much as they cost in Minnesota, she said, because the railroad and the teamsters charged so much for the hauling. The roads were so muddy that the teamsters could not haul large loads. Anyway, she made a few cents' profit on every meal, and any little bit they could earn was better than nothing.

Laura did wish she could get time to see the building that Pa was putting up. She wished she could talk to him about the building, but he ate with the boarders and hurried away with them. There was no time for talking now.

Suddenly, there on the brown prairie where nothing had been before, was the town. In two weeks, all along Main Street the unpainted new buildings pushed up their thin false fronts, two stories high and square on top. Behind the false fronts the buildings squatted under their partly shingled, sloping roofs. Strangers were already living there; smoke blew grey from the stovepipes, and glass windows glinted in the sunshine.

One day Laura heard a man say, through the clattering at the dinner table, that he was putting up a hotel. He had got in the night before with a load of lumber hauled from Brookins. His wife was coming out on the next load. 'We'll be doing business within a week,' he said.

'Glad to hear it, sir,' Pa said. 'What this town needs is a hotel. You'll be doing a land-office business, as quick as you can get started.'

As suddenly as the hurry had begun, it ended. One evening Pa and Ma and Laura and Mary and Carrie and Grace sat down to supper. No one else was there. Around them was their own house again; no one else was in it. A beautiful quiet was there, peaceful and cool, like the silence when a blizzard stops, or the restfulness of rain after a long fever of drought.

'I declare! I didn't know I was so tired,' Ma sighed peacefully.

'I'm glad you and the girls are through working for strangers,' said Pa.

They did not talk much. It was so pleasant to eat supper again alone.

'Laura and I counted up,' said Ma. 'We made over forty dollars.'

'Forty-two dollars and fifty cents,' said Laura.

'We'll put it aside and hang on to it if we can,' said Pa.

If they could save it, Laura thought, it would be that much towards sending Mary to college.

'I expect the surveyors to show up any day now,' Pa went on. 'Better be ready to move so I can turn over this house to them. We can live in town till I can sell the building.'

'Very well, Charles. We'll wash the bedding tomorrow and start getting ready to pack,' said Ma.

Next day Laura helped to wash all the quilts and blankets. She was glad to lug the loaded basket out to the clothes line in the sweet, chilly March weather. Teamsters' wagons were slowly pulling along the muddy road towards the West. Only an edging of ice remained around the shores of Silver Lake and among the dead slough grass. The lake water was blue as the sky, and far away in the shimmering sky an arrow of tiny black dots came up from the south. Faintly from far away came the wild, lonely sound of the wild geese calling.

Pa came hurrying to the house. 'First spring flock of geese's in sight!' he said. 'How about roast goose for dinner?' He hurried away with his gun.

'Mm, it will be good,' Mary said. 'Roast goose with sage stuffing! Won't you like that, Laura!'

'No, and you know I don't,' Laura answered. 'You know I don't like sage. We'll have onion in the stuffing.'

'But I don't like onion!' Mary said crossly. 'I want sage!'

Laura sat back on her heels where she was scrubbing the floor. 'I don't care if you do. We won't have it! I guess I can have what I want sometimes!'

'Why, girls!' Ma said astonished. 'Are you quarrelling?'

'I want sage!' Mary insisted.

'And I want onion!' Laura cried.

'Girls, girls,' Ma said in distress. 'I can't think what's got into you. And I never heard of anything so silly! You both know we have no sage, nor onion either.'

The door opened, and Pa came in. Soberly he put his gun in its place.

'Not a goose within gunshot,' he said. 'The whole flock rose when it came to Silver Lake and kept on going north. They must have seen the new buildings and heard the noise. Looks like hunting's going to be slim around here from now on.'

CHAPTER 27

LIVING IN TOWN

ALL around the unfinished, little town the endless prairie lay greening in the sunshine for new grass was starting everywhere. Silver Lake was blue, and the large white clouds in the sky were mirrored in the clear water.

Slowly Laura and Carrie walked on either side of Mary towards the town. Behind them came the loaded wagon, Pa and Ma and Grace riding in it, and the cow Ellen tied behind. They were all moving to Pa's building in town.

The surveyors had come back. Mr and Mrs Boast were gone to their claim. There was nowhere to live except in Pa's unfinished building, and in all the hustle, bustle and busyness of the town there was no one that Laura knew. She did not feel all alone and happy on the prairie now; she felt lonely and scared. The town's being there made the difference.

Men were busily working on the new buildings all up and down Main Street. Shavings and sawdust and ends of boards were scattered on the muddy and trampled young grass in the street, and wheels had cut deep ruts through it. Through the frames of buildings that did not have the siding on yet, and down alleys between the buildings, and beyond both ends of the street, the clean, green prairie rippled far away and quiet under the clear sky, but the town was troubled and noisy with rasping saws and pounding hammers and the thud of boxes and sharp crash of boards unloaded from wagons, and men loudly talking.

Timidly Laura and Carrie waited to let Pa's wagon come up, and they led Mary along beside it until they came to the corner where Pa's building was.

The tall false fronts loomed up, cutting off half the sky. Pa's building had a front door, with a glass window at each side. The door opened into one long room. Far at its other end was a back door, and near it a side window. The floor was wide boards, and the walls were boards with daylight coming through the cracks and knot-holes. That was all.

'This place isn't very warm nor tight, Caroline,' Pa said. 'I haven't had time to put on the siding nor to ceil the inside, and there's no cornice under the eaves to cover that big crack. But we'll be warm enough, now that spring has come, and I'll soon get the building finished.'

'You must build a stair, so we can get into the loft,' said Ma. 'Now I shall just stretch a curtain across to make two rooms so we will have a place to sleep until you can put up a partition. Warm as this weather is, we don't need siding and ceiling.'

Pa put Ellen and the horses in a small stable at the back of the lot. Then he set up the stove and stretched a rope for Ma's curtain. Ma hung sheets on it while Laura helped Pa set up the bedstead. Then Carrie helped her make the beds while Mary amused Grace and Ma got supper.

The lamplight shone on the white curtain while they ate, but the end of the long room was shadowy and the chilly air coming through all the cracks made the lamp flicker and the curtain move. There was too much empty space in that building but all the time Laura felt that strangers were close outside it. Lamplight shone out of strangers' windows, footsteps passed with a lantern, and voices were talking though she could not hear the words. Even when the night was still, she felt crowded by so many other people so near. She lay in bed with Mary in the dark and airy room, and stared at the vague white curtain and listened to the stillness and felt trapped in town.

Sometime in the night she dreamed of wolves' howling, but she was in bed and the howling was only the wind. She was cold. She was too cold to wake up. The covers seemed very thin. She snuggled closer to Mary and burrowed her cold head under the thin covers. In her sleep she was tight and shivering, till finally she grew cosily warm. The next she knew, she heard Pa singing.

> 'Oh, I am as happy as a big sunflower
>   That nods and bends in the breezes!
> And my heart is as light as the wind that blows
>   The leaves from off the treeses!'

Laura opened one eye and peeked from under the covers. Snow fell softly on to her face, a great lot of snow.

'Ow!' she said.

'Lie still, Laura!' said Pa. 'All you girls lie still. I'll

shovel you out in a minute. Soon as I get this fire started and the snow off Ma.'

Laura heard the stove lids clatter. She heard the scratch of a match and the crackle of burning kindling. She did not stir. The covers were heavy over her and she was warm as toast.

Soon Pa came behind the curtain. 'There's a good foot of snow on these beds!' he exclaimed. 'But I'll have it off in three jerks of a lamb's tail. Lie still now, girls!'

Laura and Mary lay perfectly still, while Pa shovelled the snow off their covers, and the cold came through them. They lay shivering and watching while with his shovel he took the snow off Carrie and Grace. Then he went to the stable to shovel out Ellen and the horses.

'Get up, girls!' Ma called. 'Bring your clothes and dress by the fire.'

Laura jumped out of the warm bed and grabbed her clothes from the chair where she had laid them the night before. She shook the snow off them and ran barefoot over snow scattered on the cold floor, to the stove beyond the curtain. As she ran she said, 'Wait, Mary. I'll come back in a minute and shake the snow off your clothes.'

She shook out her petticoats and her dress so quickly that the snow had no time to melt on them. Quickly she shook her stockings and emptied the snow from her shoes, and put them on. She hurried so fast that when she was dressed she was quite warm. Then she shook the snow from Mary's clothes and helped her quickly to the warmth that the oven gave out.

Carrie came running with little squeals and jumps. 'Oo, the snow burns my feet!' she said, laughing though her teeth chattered from cold. It was so exciting to wake up in a snowdrift that she wouldn't wait in bed until Laura could shake her clothes. Laura helped button her up, then they put on their coats, and with the stove shovel and the broom they scooped and swept back the snow into piles in the far corners of the long room.

Snow lay in piles and drifts all along the street. Every lumber pile was a mountain of snow, and from the drifts the bare timbers of unfinished buildings stuck up thin and yellow. The sun was up, and all the slopes of snow were rosy and all the hollows blue. Through every crack the air came in as cold as ice.

Ma warmed her shawl by the fire, wrapped it snugly around Grace, and brought her to Mary, in the rocking-chair pulled close to the oven. The hot stove made the air fairly warm all around it. Ma set the table almost against the stove, and breakfast was ready when Pa came back.

'This building's a pretty good sieve!' Pa said. 'Snow blew through every crack and in under the eaves. That was a genuine blizzard while it lasted.'

'To think we went all winter without a blizzard, and now we get one in April,' Ma marvelled.

'Lucky it struck in the night when folks were under cover,' said Pa. 'If it had hit in the daytime, somebody would have been lost and frozen sure. Nobody looks for a blizzard at this time of year.'

'Well, the cold can't last long,' Ma encouraged herself. ' "April showers bring May flowers." What will an April blizzard bring?'

'For one thing, a partition,' said Pa. 'I'll have a partition up to keep in the heat around this stove before I'm a day older.'

And he did. All day by the stove he sawed and hammered. Laura and Carrie helped hold the boards, and in Mary's lap Grace played with the shavings. The new partition made a little room, with the stove and the table and the beds in it, and its window looking out at all the green prairie covered with snow.

Then Pa brought in more snowy lumber and he began

ceiling the walls. 'I'll stop some of the cracks anyway,' he said.

All over the town there was sawing and hammering inside the other buildings. Ma said, 'I'm sorry for Mrs Beardsley, keeping a hotel while it's being built over her head.'

'That's what it takes to build up a country,' said Pa. 'Building over your head and under your feet, but building. We'd never get anything fixed to suit us if we waited for things to suit us before we started.'

In a few days the snow was gone and spring came back again. The wind from the prairie brought a smell of damp ground and young grass, the sun rose earlier every day, and faintly all day the blue sky clanged with the wild birds' calls. High in the sky Laura could see them flying, flock after flock dark and small in the shimmering air.

They did not gather thickly any more on Silver Lake. Only a few very tired flocks settled late after sunset in the sloughs and rose to the sky again before the sun rose. Wild birds did not like the town full of people, and neither did Laura.

She thought, 'I would rather be out on the prairie with the grass and the birds and Pa's fiddle. Yes, even with wolves! I would rather be anywhere than in this muddy, cluttered, noisy town, crowded by strange people.' And she said, 'Pa, when are we going to move to the homestead?'

'Soon as I sell this building,' said Pa.

More and more wagons came in every day. Teams and wagons pulled along the muddy street, past the windows. All day there was the noise of hammers and of boots and voices. The shovel gangs were levelling the railroad grade, the teamsters were unloading ties and steel rails. In the evenings they were loudly drinking in the saloons.

Carrie liked the town. She wanted to go out into it and see everything, and for hours she stood looking out of the windows. Sometimes Ma let her cross the street to visit two little girls who lived there, but oftener the little girls came to see her, for Ma did not like to let Carrie out of her sight.

'I declare, Laura, you are so restless you give me the fidgets,' Ma said one day. 'You are going to teach school, so why not begin now? Don't you think it would be nice if you taught Carrie and Louizy and Annie every day? It would keep Carrie at home and be good for you all.'

Laura did not think it would be nice. She did not want to do it at all. But she said obediently, 'Yes, Ma.'

She thought she might as well try. So next morning when Louizy and Annie came to play with Carrie, Laura told them that they would have a school. She seated them all in a row and set them a lesson to study in Ma's old primer.

'You study that for fifteen minutes,' she told them, 'and then I will hear you.'

They looked at her with wide eyes, but they did not say anything. They put their heads together and studied, while Laura sat in front of them. There never was such a long fifteen minutes. At last Laura heard their spelling lesson, and then she set them a lesson in arithmetic. Whenever they fidgeted she told them they must sit still, and she made them raise their hands for permission to speak.

'You all did very nicely, I'm sure,' Ma smiled in approval, when at last it was time to get dinner. 'You may come every morning, and Laura will teach you. Tell your mother I shall step across the street this afternoon and tell her about our little school.'

'Yes, ma'am,' Louizy and Annie answered weakly. 'Good-bye, ma'am.'

'With diligence and perseverance, Laura, I think you will be a very good teacher,' Ma praised Laura, and Laura answered, 'Thank you, Ma.' She thought, 'I've got to be a teacher, so I might as well try hard to be a good one.'

Every morning little brown-haired Annie and red-headed Louizy came more reluctantly; every day it was harder to teach them. They fidgeted so that Laura despaired of ever making them sit still, and she could not make them study. One day they did not come.

'Perhaps they are too young to appreciate schooling, but I wonder at their mother,' said Ma.

'Don't be discouraged, Laura,' Mary said. 'Anyway, you have taught the first school in De Smet.'

'I'm not discouraged,' Laura said cheerfully. She was so glad to be free from teaching that she began to sing while she swept the floor.

From the window Carrie cried out, 'Look, Laura! Something's happening! Maybe that's why they don't come.'

In front of the hotel a crowd was gathering. More and more men came from all directions, and the sound of their voices was loud and excited. Laura remembered the payday crowd that had threatened Pa. In a minute she saw Pa breaking through the crowd and coming home.

He came in looking sober. 'What do you say to moving out to the claim right away, Caroline?' he asked.

'Today?' Ma asked.

'Day after tomorrow,' said Pa. 'It will take me that long to put up a claim shanty.'

'Sit down, Charles, and tell me what is wrong,' Ma said quietly.

Pa sat down. 'There's been a murder.'

Ma's eyes opened wide and she caught her breath. She said, 'Here?'

'South of town.' Pa got up. 'A claim jumper killed Hunter. He used to work on the grade. He drove out yesterday to his homestead, he and his father. When they drove up to his claim shanty, a man opened the door and looked out at them. Hunter asked him what he was doing there, and he shot Hunter dead. He tried to shoot the old man, but he whipped up the team and got away. Neither one of them had a gun. The old man got to Mitchell and brought officers out this morning, and they arrested the fellow. Arrested him!' Pa said furiously. 'Hanging's too good for him. If we'd only known in time!'

'Charles,' Ma said.

'Well,' said Pa, 'I think we'd better get on to our claim before somebody jumps it.'

'So do I,' Ma agreed. 'We will move as soon as you can put up any kind of shelter.'

'Fix me up a snack to eat, and I'll start now,' said Pa. 'I'll go get a load of lumber and a man to help and put up the shanty this afternoon. We'll move tomorrow.'

CHAPTER 28

MOVING DAY

'WAKE up, sleepyhead!' Laura sang out, and with both hands she rolled Carrie back and forth under the quilts. 'It's moving day! Get up quick, we're moving to the homestead!'

Quickly they all ate breakfast, wasting no time in talk, and quickly Laura washed the dishes and Carrie dried them, while Ma packed the last box and Pa hitched up the team. This was the gladdest moving day that Laura had known. Ma and Mary were glad because this was the end of travelling; they were going to settle on the homestead and never move again. Carrie was glad because she was eager to see the homestead, Laura was glad because they were leaving town, Pa was glad because he always liked moving, and Grace sang and shouted in gladness because all the others were glad.

As fast as the dishes were wiped, Ma packed them in the tub so they would ride safely. Pa loaded the trunk, the packed boxes and the tub of dishes into the wagon. Then Ma helped him take down the stove-pipe, and they put it and the stove into the wagon box. He laid the table and the chairs on top of all, and then he looked at the load and tugged his beard.

'I'll have to make two trips so we can all ride,' he said. 'Get the rest of the stuff ready and I'll be back.'

'But you can't unload the stove by yourself,' Ma objected.

'I'll manage,' said Pa. 'What goes up must come down, and I'll rig up some skids; there's lumber out there.'

He climbed into the wagon and drove away. Then Ma and Laura rolled the bedding into tight rolls. They took down Ma's big bedstead and the two smaller new bedsteads that Pa had bought in town, and they packed the lamps carefully in a box, right side up so that they would not spill the kerosene. They stuffed the lamp chimneys with paper and wrapped them in towels and packed them beside the lamps. Everything was ready and waiting before Pa came back.

He put the bedstead and the boxes in the wagon, and laid the rolls of bedding on them. Then Laura handed him the fiddle box and he tucked it carefully among the quilts. On top of all he laid the whatnot, on its back so that it could not be scratched. Then he brought Ellen and tied her behind the wagon.

'Now, Caroline, up you go!' He handed Ma over the

wagon wheel to the spring seat. 'Catch!' and he tossed Grace into Ma's lap. 'Now, Mary,' he said gently, and he helped her to the board laid close behind the seat, while Laura and Carrie clambered to their places beside her.

'Now then,' said Pa, 'we will soon be home.'

'For pity's sake, Laura, put on your sunbonnet!' Ma exclaimed. 'This spring wind will ruin your complexion.' And she pulled Grace's little bonnet farther forward to protect her fair, soft skin. Mary's face was far back in her bonnet, and so was Ma's, of course.

Slowly Laura pulled up her own bonnet by its strings, from where it hung down her back, and as its slatted sides came past her cheeks they shut out the town. From the tunnel of the bonnet she saw only the green prairie and blue sky.

She kept on looking at them, while she held on to the back of the spring seat and joggled to the wagon's jolting over the wind-dried ruts of mud. While she was looking, suddenly into the sunny green and blue came two brown horses with flowing black manes and tails, trotting side by side in harness. Their brown flanks and shoulders gleamed in the sunshine, their slender legs stepped daintily, their necks were arched and their ears pricked up, and they tossed their heads proudly as they went by.

'Oh, what beautiful horses!' Laura cried. 'Look, Pa! Look!' She turned her head to watch them as long as she could. They drew a light wagon. A young man stood up in the wagon, driving, and a taller man stood behind him with a hand on his shoulder. In a moment the backs of the men and the wagon loomed up so that Laura could no longer see the horses.

Pa had turned around in the seat to watch them too. 'Those are the Wilder boys,' he said. 'Almanzo's driving, and that's his brother Royal with him. They've taken up claims north of town, and they've got the finest horses in this whole country. By George, you seldom see a team like that.'

With all her heart Laura wished for such horses. She supposed she never could have them.

Pa was driving south now, across the green prairie and down a gentle slope towards Big Slough. The ranker, coarse grass of the slough filled its straggling hollow, and up from a water pool flapped a heron with dangling long legs.

'How much do they cost, Pa?' Laura asked.

'What, Flutterbudget?' said Pa.

'Horses like those.'

'A matched team like that? Not a penny under two hundred and fifty dollars, maybe three hundred,' said Pa. 'Why?'

'Nothing. I was just wondering,' Laura replied. Three hundred dollars was so much money that she could hardly imagine it. Only rich people could pay such a sum for horses. Laura thought that if ever she were rich, what she would have would be two sleek brown horses with black manes and tails. She let her bonnet fly back in the wind and thought of riding behind such fast horses.

Far to the west and south, Big Slough widened and spread. On the other side of the wagon it ran narrow and marshy to the narrow tip of Silver Lake. Quickly Pa drove across the narrow part and up to the higher ground beyond.

'There it is!' he said. The little claim shanty stood bright in its newness in the sunlight. It looked like a yellow toy on the great rolling prairie covered with rippling young grass.

Ma laughed at it when Pa helped her from the wagon. 'It looks like half a woodshed that has been split in two.'

'You are wrong, Caroline,' Pa told her. 'It is a little house only half built, and that half unfinished. We'll finish it now, and build the other half soon.'

The little house and its half a slanting roof were built

of rough boards with cracks between. There were no windows and no door for the doorway, but there was a floor. And a trap door in the floor opened into a cellar.

'I couldn't do more than dig the cellar and put up rough walls yesterday,' said Pa. 'But now we're here! Nobody can jump our claim. And I'll soon fix things up for you, Caroline.'

'I'm glad to be home, Charles,' said Ma.

Before sunset they were all settled in the funny little house. The stove was up, the beds were made, the curtain was hung to make two tiny rooms of the one small room. Supper was cooked and eaten, the dishes washed, and darkness was falling softly on the prairie. No one wanted the lamp lighted, the spring night was so beautiful.

Ma sat gently rocking by the doorless doorway, holding Grace in her lap and Carrie close beside her. Mary and Laura sat together on the threshold. Pa sat just outside the doorway, in a chair on the grass. They did not talk. They sat looking, while stars came out one by one and frogs were croaking in the Big Slough.

A little wind was whispering. The darkness was velvety soft and quiet and safe. All over the huge sky the stars were twinkling merrily.

Then Pa said softly, 'I feel like music, Laura.'

Laura brought the fiddle box from its safe place under Ma's bed. Pa took the fiddle from its nest and tuned it lovingly. Then they sang to the night and the stars:

'Oh, drive dull care away,
  For weeping is but sorrow.
  If things are wrong today,
  There's another day tomorrow.

'So drive dull care away
  And do the best you can.
  Put your shoulder to the wheel
  Is the motto for every man.'

'I am going to put up the little shepherdess just as soon as the roof is finished over our heads,' said Ma.

Pa's fiddle answered her with little notes running like water in the sunshine and widening into a pool. The moon was rising. The creamy light crept up the sky and the stars melted in it. Cool and silvery, the moonlight lay over the wide, dark land, and softly Pa sang with the fiddle:

> 'When the stars are brightly beaming
> And the sighing winds are still,
> When the twilight shadows hover o'er the lea,
> There's a tiny candle gleaming
> From the cottage 'neath the hill
> And I know that little beacon shines for me.'

CHAPTER 29

THE SHANTY ON THE CLAIM

'THE first thing to do is to dig a well,' said Pa next morning. He shouldered his spade and shovel and went whistling towards the slough while Laura cleared the breakfast table and Ma rolled up her sleeves.

'Now girls,' she said cheerfully, 'all together with a will, and we'll soon have things to rights.'

But even Ma was puzzled that morning. The little claim shanty was as full as it would hold. Everything must be carefully fitted into the space. Laura and Carrie and Ma lifted and tugged the furniture this way and that, and stood and thought, and tried again. Mary's rocking-chair and the table were still outdoors when Pa came back.

'Well, Caroline, your well's all dug!' he sang out. 'Six feet deep, and good, cold water in quicksand. Now I'll hammer together a cover for it, so Grace can't fall in, and that'll be done.' He looked at the disorder and pushed back his hat to scratch his head. 'Can't you get it all in?'

'Yes, Charles,' said Ma. 'Where there's a will, there's a way.'

It was Laura who thought how to fit in the beds. The trouble was that they now had three bedsteads. When they stood side by side, there was not room for Mary's rocking-chair. Laura thought of setting the little bedsteads together, tight in the corner, and putting the foot of the big bedstead against them, with its headboard against the other wall.

'Then we'll hang a curtain around our beds,' she said to Ma, 'and another curtain across beside yours, and that leaves room for the rocking-chair against your curtain.'

'That's my smart girl!' said Ma.

Against the foot of Laura's and Mary's bed, the table fitted under the window that Pa was sawing in that wall. Ma's rocking-chair went in beside the table, and the what-not fitted in that corner, behind the door. In the fourth corner stood the stove, with the dish cupboard made of a packing box behind it, and the trunk fitted between the stove and Mary's rocking-chair.

'There!' said Ma. 'And the boxes will go under the beds. It couldn't be better!'

At dinner Pa said, 'Before night I'll finish this half of a house.' And he did. He put in a window beside the stove, to the south. He hung in the doorway a door bought from the lumberyard in town. Then all over the outside of the shanty he put black tar paper, fastening it down with lath.

Laura helped him unroll the wide, black, tarry-smelling paper down over the slanting roof and the walls of fresh, clean, pine-scented boards, and she helped him cut it and she held it down in the wind while he nailed on the lath. Tar-paper was not pretty, but it stopped all the cracks and kept out the wind.

'Well, there's one good day's work done,' Pa said when they sat down to supper.

'Yes,' said Ma. 'And tomorrow we'll finish unpacking and be finally settled. I must do a baking too. It's a blessing to have yeast once more. I feel as though I never want to see another sour-dough biscuit.'

'Your light bread is good and so are your sour-dough biscuits,' Pa told her. 'But we won't have either if I don't rustle something to bake them with. Tomorrow I'll haul a load of wood from Lake Henry.'

'May I go with you, Pa?' Laura asked.

'Me, too?' Carrie begged.

'No, girls,' said Pa. 'I'll be gone quite a while and Ma will need you.'

'I wanted to see trees,' Carrie explained.

'I don't blame her,' said Ma. 'I would like to see some trees again myself. They would rest my eyes from all this prairie with not a tree. Not even a bush to be seen in any direction.'

'This country's going to be covered with trees,' Pa said. 'Don't forget that Uncle Sam's tending to that. There's a tree claim on every section, and settlers have got to plant ten acres of trees on every tree claim. In four or five years you'll see trees every way you look.'

'I'll be looking in all directions at once then,' Ma smiled. 'There's nothing more restful than shady groves in the summertime, and they'll break the wind too.'

'Well, I don't know,' said Pa. 'Trees spread, and you know what it was like back in the Big Woods of Wisconsin, grubbing out stumps and breaking our backs on the sprouting hoe to keep a little land clear for crops. It's restful to have clear prairie land like this, if you're going to farm. But Uncle Sam don't seem to look at it that way, so don't worry, Caroline; you're going to see plenty of trees all over this country. Likely they'll stop the wind and change the climate, too, just as you say.'

They were all too tired for music that night. Soon after supper they were all asleep, and bright and early next morning Pa drove away towards Lake Henry.

The whole world was gay in the early sunshine when Laura led Ellen to drink at the well. All over the prairie the little white blossoms of wild onion were dancing in the wind. Down the slope of the little hill below the shanty, patches of wild crocus spread yellow and blue in the young grass, and everywhere the sheep-sorrel uncurled its little pink-lavender flowers above sleek clover-shaped leaves. Laura bent down to pick them as she walked, and slowly nibbled the delightfully fresh, sour little stems and petals.

From the grassy swell where she picketed Ellen she could see the town beyond to the north. Big Slough curved between and spread wide south-west, covering acres upon acres with its rough high grass. All the rest of the whole enormous prairie was a green carpet flowered with spring blossoms.

Big girl as she was, Laura spread her arms wide to the wind and ran against it. She flung herself on the flowery grass and rolled like a colt. She lay in the soft, sweet grasses and looked at the great blueness above her and the high, pearly clouds sailing in it. She was so happy that tears came into her eyes.

Suddenly she thought, 'Have I got a grass stain on my dress?' She stood up and anxiously looked, and there was a green stain on the calico. Soberly she knew that she should be helping Ma, and she hurried to the little dark tar-paper shanty.

'It's tiger-striped,' she said to Ma.

'What is, Laura?' Ma asked, looking up startled. She was putting her books on the bottom shelves of the whatnot.

'This shanty,' said Laura. 'Striped with yellow lath on the tar paper.'

'Tigers are yellow with black stripes,' Mary objected.

'You girls unpack your boxes now,' said Ma. 'We'll arrange all our pretty things on these upper shelves.'

On the shelf above the books there was room for Mary's and Laura's and Carrie's little glass boxes. Each box had frosted flowers on its side and coloured flowers on the lid. The three made that shelf all bright and gay.

Ma stood the clock on the fourth shelf. Its brown wooden case spread up in a carved lacy pattern from its round glass face, and behind glass painted with gilt flowers its brass pendulum wagged to and fro, tick-tock, tick-tock.

On the smallest, very top shelf above the clock, Laura set her white china jewel box with the tiny gold cup and saucer on its top, and Carrie put beside it her brown-and-white china dog.

'It's very pretty, I'm sure,' Ma approved. 'When the door is shut, the whatnot quite dresses up the room. Now for the china shepherdess.' Then she looked around quickly and exclaimed, 'Mercy! Is my bread-sponge risen already?'

The bread-sponge was lifting the lid of the pan. Ma hurriedly floured the breadboard, and kneaded the dough. Then she got dinner. She was putting the pan of light biscuits in the oven when Pa came driving the wagon up the hill. Behind him the wagon box was piled high with willow brush that he had brought for summer fuel, for there were no real trees at Lake Henry.

'Hello, Flutterbudget! Let dinner wait, Caroline!' he called. 'I've got something to show you as soon as I picket the team.'

Quickly he slipped the harness off the horses and

dumped it across the wagon tongue. He hurried the horses away to their picket ropes, and came hurrying back. Then he lifted a horse blanket from the front of the wagon box.

'There you are, Caroline!' he beamed. 'I covered them so they wouldn't dry out in the wind.'

'What, Charles?' Ma and Laura craned to see into the wagon box, and Carrie climbed up the wheel. 'Trees!' Ma exclaimed.

'Little trees!' Laura shouted. 'Mary! Pa's brought little trees!'

'They're cottonwoods,' Pa said. 'They all grew from seeds of the Lone Tree that we saw across the prairie when we were coming out from Brookins. It's a giant of a tree when you get close to it. It's seeded all along the edge of Lake Henry. I dug enough of these seedlings to make a windbreak clear around the shanty. You're going to have your trees growing, Caroline, quick as I can get them set in the ground.'

He took his spade out of the wagon and said, 'The first one's your tree, Caroline. Pick it out and tell me where you want it.'

'Just a minute,' Ma answered. She hurried to the stove and shut its draught and set back the pot of potatoes. Then she picked out her tree. 'I want it right here by the door,' she said.

With his spade, Pa cut a square in the sod and lifted the grass. He dug a hole and loosened the soft soil until it was fine and crumbly. Then carefully he lifted the little tree and carried it without shaking the earth from its roots.

'Hold the top straight, Caroline,' he said. Ma held the small tree straight by its top, while with his spade Pa sifted earth over its roots until the hole was filled. Then he stamped the earth down firmly, and stood back. 'Now you can look at a tree, Caroline. Your own tree. We'll give each one of 'em a pailful of water after dinner. But first we'll get their roots in the ground. Come, Mary, it's your turn next.'

Pa dug another hole in a straight line with the first. He brought another tree from the wagon, and Mary carefully held it upright while Pa planted it. That was Mary's tree.

'Yours is next, Laura,' said Pa. 'We'll make a square windbreak, all around the house. Ma's tree and mine by the door, and a tree for each of you girls on each side of ours.'

Laura held her tree while Pa planted it. Then Carrie held hers. The four little trees stood up straight from the patches of dark earth in the grass.

'Now Grace must have hers,' said Pa. 'Where's Grace?' He called to Ma, 'Caroline, bring Grace out here to plant her tree!'

Ma looked out of the shanty. 'She's out there with you, Charles,' she said.

'I guess she's behind the house, I'll get her,' Carrie said, and she ran, calling, 'Grace!' In a minute she came from behind the shanty, her eyes large and scared and the freckles standing out from her pale face. 'Pa, I can't find her!'

'She must be close by,' said Ma, and she called, 'Grace! Grace!' Pa shouted too, 'Grace!'

'Don't stand there! Go look for her, Carrie! Laura, go!' Ma said. She exclaimed, 'The well!' and ran down the path.

The cover was on the well, so Grace had not fallen into it.

'She can't be lost,' Pa said.

'I left her outdoors. I thought she was with you,' said Ma.

'She can't be lost,' Pa insisted. 'She wasn't out of my sight a minute.' He shouted, 'Grace! Grace!'

Laura ran panting up the hill. She could not see Grace

anywhere. Along the edge of the Big Slough towards Silver Lake she looked, and over the flowery prairie. Quickly, quickly she looked, again and again, seeing nothing but wild flowers and grasses. 'Grace! Grace!' she screamed. 'Grace!'

Pa met her on the slope as she ran down and Ma came up gasping for breath. 'She must be in sight, Laura,' Pa said. 'You must have missed seeing her. She can't be –' Terribly he exclaimed, 'The Big Slough!' He turned and ran.

Ma ran after him, calling back, 'Carrie, you stay with Mary! Laura, look for her, go look!'

Mary stood in the doorway of the shanty calling, 'Grace! Grace!' More faintly from Big Slough came Pa's shouts and Ma's, 'Grace! Where are you? Grace!'

If Grace was lost in the Big Slough, how could anyone find her? The old, dead grass stood higher than Laura's head, over acres and acres, for miles and miles. The deep mud sucked at bare feet, and there were water holes. Laura could hear, where she stood, the sound of the coarse slough grass in the wind, a muffling sound that almost smothered even Ma's shrill call, 'Grace!'

Laura felt cold and sick.

'Why don't you look for her?' Carrie cried. 'Don't stand there! Do something! I'm going myself!'

'Ma told you to stay with Mary,' said Laura. 'So you'd better stay.'

'She told you to look!' Carrie screamed. 'Go look! Go look! Grace! Grace!'

'Shut up! Let me think!' Laura screeched, and she started running across the sunny prairie.

CHAPTER 30

WHERE VIOLETS GROW

LAURA was running straight towards the south. Grass whipped soft against her bare feet. Butterflies fluttered over the flowers. There wasn't a bush nor a weed that Grace could be hidden behind. There was nothing, nothing but grass and flowers swaying in the sunshine.

If she were little and playing all by herself, Laura thought, she wouldn't go into the dark Big Slough, she wouldn't go into the mud and the tall grass. Oh, Grace, why didn't I watch you? she thought. Sweet pretty little helpless sister – 'Grace! Grace!' she screamed. Her breath caught and hurt in her side.

She ran on and on. Grace must have gone this way. Maybe she chased a butterfly. She didn't go into Big Slough! She didn't climb the hill, she wasn't there. Oh, baby sister, I couldn't see you anywhere east or south on this hateful prairie. 'Grace!'

The horrible, sunny prairie was so large. No lost baby could ever be found on it. Ma's calling and Pa's shouts came from Big Slough. They were thin cries, lost in wind, lost on the enormous bigness of the prairie.

Laura's breathing hurt her sides under the ribs. Her chest was smothering and her eyes were dizzy. She ran up a low slope. Nothing, nothing, not a spot of shadow was anywhere on the level prairie all around her. She ran on, and suddenly the ground dropped before her. She almost fell down a steep bank.

There was Grace. There, in a great pool of blue, sat Grace. The sun shone on her golden hair blowing in the wind. She looked up at Laura with big eyes as blue as violets. Her hands were full of violets. She held them up to Laura and said, 'Sweet! Sweet!'

Laura sank down and took Grace in her arms. She held Grace carefully and panted for breath. Grace leaned over her arm to reach more violets. They were surrounded by masses of violets blossoming above low-spreading leaves. Violets covered the flat bottom of a large, round hollow. All around this lake of violets, grassy banks rose almost straight up to the prairie-level. There in the round, low place the wind hardly disturbed the fragrance of the violets. The sun was warm there, the sky was overhead, the green walls of grass curved all around, and butterflies fluttered over the crowding violet-faces.

Laura stood up and lifted Grace to her feet. She took

the violets that Grace gave her, and clasped her hand. 'Come, Grace,' she said. 'We must go home.'

She gave one look around the little hollow while she helped Grace climb the bank.

Grace walked so slowly that for a little while Laura carried her. Then she let her walk, for Grace was nearly three years old, and heavy. Then she lifted her again. So, carrying Grace and helping her walk, Laura brought her to the shanty and gave her to Mary.

Then she ran towards the Big Slough, calling as she ran. 'Pa! Ma! She's here!' She kept on calling until Pa heard her and shouted to Ma, far in the tall grass. Slowly, together, they fought their way out of Big Slough and slowly came up to the shanty, draggled and muddy and very tired and thankful.

'Where did you find her, Laura?' Ma asked, taking Grace in her arms and sinking into her chair.

'In a –' Laura hesitated, and said, 'Pa, could it really be a fairy ring? It is perfectly round. The bottom is perfectly flat. The bank around it is the same height all the way. You can't see a sign of that place till you stand on the bank. It is very large, and the whole bottom of it is covered solidly thick with violets. A place like that couldn't just happen, Pa. Something made it.'

'You are too old to be believing in fairies, Laura,' Ma said gently. 'Charles, you must not encourage such fancies.'

'But it isn't – it isn't like a real place, truly,' Laura protested. 'And smell how sweet the violets are. They aren't like ordinary violets.'

'They do make the whole house sweet,' Ma admitted. 'But they are real violets, and there are no fairies.'

'You are right, Laura; human hands didn't make that place,' Pa said. 'But your fairies were big, ugly brutes, with horns on their heads and humps on their backs. That place is an old buffalo wallow. You know buffaloes are wild cattle. They paw up the ground and wallow in the dust, just as cattle do.

'For ages the buffalo herds had these wallowing places. They pawed up the ground and the wind blew the dust away. Then another herd came along and pawed up more dust in the same place. They went always to the same places, and –'

'Why did they, Pa?' Laura asked.

'I don't know,' Pa said. 'Maybe because the ground was mellowed there. Now the buffalo are gone, and grass grows over their wallows. Grass and violets.'

'Well,' Ma said. 'All's well that ends well, and here it is long past dinner-time. I hope you and Carrie didn't let the biscuits burn, Mary.'

'No, Ma,' Mary said, and Carrie showed her the biscuits wrapped in a clean cloth to keep warm, and the potatoes drained and mealy-dry in their pot. And Laura said, 'Sit still, Ma, and rest. I'll fry the salt pork and make the gravy.'

No one but Grace was hungry. They ate slowly, and then Pa finished planting the windbreak. Ma helped Grace hold her own little tree while Pa set it firmly. When all the trees were planted, Carrie and Laura gave them each a full pail of water from the well. Before they finished, it was time to help get supper.

'Well,' Pa said at the table. 'We're settled at last on our homestead claim.'

'Yes,' said Ma. 'All but one thing. Mercy, what a day this has been. I didn't get time to drive the nail for the bracket.'

'I'll tend to it, Caroline, as soon as I drink my tea,' Pa said.

He took the hammer from his toolbox under the bed, and drove a nail into the wall between the table and the whatnot. 'Now bring on your bracket and the china shepherdess!' he said.

Ma brought them to him. He hung the bracket on the nail and stood the china shepherdess on its shelf. Her little china shoes, her tight china bodice and her golden hair were as bright as they had been so long ago in the Big Woods. Her china skirts were as wide and white; her cheeks as pink and her blue eyes as sweet as ever. And the bracket that Pa had carved for Ma's Christmas present so long ago was still without a scratch, and even more glossily polished than when it was new.

Over the door Pa hung his rifle and his shotgun, and then he hung on a nail above them a bright, new horseshoe.

'Well,' he said, looking around at the snugly crowded shanty. 'A short horse is soon curried. This is our tightest squeeze yet, Caroline, but it's only a beginning.' Ma's eyes smiled into his eyes, and he said to Laura, 'I could sing you a song about that horseshoe.'

She brought him the fiddle box, and he sat down in the doorway and tuned the fiddle. Ma settled in her chair to rock Grace to sleep. Softly Laura washed the dishes and Carrie wiped them while Pa played the fiddle and sang.

> 'We journey along quite contented in life
>   And try to live peaceful with all.
> We keep ourselves free from all trouble and strife
>   And we're glad when our friends on us call.
> Our hope it is happy and cheerful and bright,
>   We're content and we ask nothing more.
> And the reason we prosper, I'll tell to you now,
>   There's a horseshoe hung over the door!

> 'Keep the horseshoe hung over the door!
>   It will bring you good luck evermore.
> If you would be happy and free from all care,
>   Keep the horseshoe hung over the door!'

'It sounds rather heathenish to me, Charles,' Ma said.

'Well, anyway,' Pa replied, 'I wouldn't wonder if we do pretty well here, Caroline. In time we'll build more rooms on this house, and maybe have a driving team and buggy. I'm not going to plough up much grass. We'll have a garden and a little field, but mostly raise hay and cattle. Where so many buffalo ranged, must be a good country for cattle.'

The dishes were done. Laura carried the dishpan some distance from the back door and flung the water far over the grass where tomorrow's sun would dry it. The first stars were pricking through the pale sky. A few lights twinkled yellow in the little town, but the whole great plain of earth was shadowy. There was hardly a wind, but the air moved and whispered to itself in the grasses. Laura almost knew what it said. Lonely and wild and eternal were land and water and sky and the air blowing.

'The buffalo are gone,' Laura thought. 'And now we're homesteaders.'

CHAPTER 31

MOSQUITOES

'WE must build a stable for the horses,' Pa said. 'It won't always be warm enough for them to stay outdoors and a bad storm might come even in summer. They must have shelter.'

'Ellen too, Pa?' Laura asked.

'Cattle are better off outdoors in the summer,' Pa told her. 'But I like to have horses in a stable at night.'

Laura held boards for Pa. She handed him tools and brought nails while he built the stable, at the west of the house against the little hill. It would be sheltered there on the west and the north, when the cold winter winds were blowing.

The days were warm. Mosquitoes came out of the Big Slough at sundown and sang their high, keen song all night as they swarmed around Ellen, biting her and sucking the blood until she ran around and around on her picket rope. They went into the stable and bit the horses until they pulled at their halters and stamped. They came into the claim shanty and bit everyone there until great blotches raised on faces and hands.

Their singing and the sting of their bites made night a torment.

'This will never do,' Pa said. 'We must have mosquito bar on the windows and door.'

'It's the Big Slough,' Ma complained. 'The mosquitoes come from there. I wish we were farther away from it.'

But Pa liked the Big Slough. 'There are acres and acres of hay there, that anyone can have for the cutting,' he told Ma. 'No one will ever take up homesteads in the Big Slough. There is only upland hay on our place, but with the Big Slough so near, we can always cut hay there and have all we need.

'Besides, all the prairie grass is full of mosquitoes too. I'll go to town today and get some mosquito bar.'

Pa brought yards of pink mosquito bar from town and strips of lumber to make a frame for a screen door.

While he made the door, Ma tacked mosquito bar over the windows. Then she tacked it to the door frame and Pa hung the screen door.

That night he built a smudge of old, damp grass, so the smoke would drift before the stable door. Mosquitoes would not go through the smoke.

Pa made another smudge so Ellen could stand in its smoke and she went at once and stayed there.

Pa made sure there was no dry grass near the smudges and built them up so they would last all night.

'There!' he said, 'I guess that fixes the mosquitoes.'

CHAPTER 32

EVENING SHADOWS FALL

SAM and David stood quietly, resting in the stable, with the smoke screen before the door.

Ellen, on her picket rope, lay comfortably in the smoke from the smudge. No mosquitoes could get at them.

There was not one of the singing pests inside the claim shanty. They could not come through the mosquito bar over the door and windows.

'Now we are all snug,' Pa said, 'settled at last on our homestead. Bring me the fiddle, Laura, and we'll have a little music!'

Grace was safely in her bed with Carrie beside her.

Ma and Mary sat rocking gently in the shadows. But moonlight shone through the southern window and touched Pa's face and hands and the fiddle as the bow moved smoothly over the strings.

Laura sat near Mary and watched it as she thought how

the moonlight would be shining in the fairy ring where the violets grew. It was just the night for fairies to be dancing there.

Pa was singing with the fiddle:

'In Scarlet town where I was born,
  There was a fair maid dwellin';
  And every youth cried "Well-a-wa."
  Her name was Barbary Allen.

'All in the merry month of May,
  When green buds they were swellin'
  Young Johnnie Grove on his death bed lay
  For love of Barbary Allen.'

Laura drew the curtain as she and Mary joined Carrie and Grace in their tiny bedroom.

And, as she fell asleep still thinking of violets and fairy rings and moonlight over the wide, wide land, where their very own homestead lay, Pa and the fiddle were softly singing:

'Home! Home! Sweet, sweet home,
  Be it ever so humble
  There is no place like home.'

Also by Laura Ingalls Wilder

THE LONG WINTER

The fifth book about Laura's adventures tells of the year when Laura was fourteen and the family were all settled on Pa's claim in Dakota, when something went wrong with the weather. The animals knew it first. Every kind of bird was flying south as fast as it could, and every thing that runs or swims was hidden away. 'I don't like it,' Pa said, slowly shaking his head. 'I don't like the feel of the weather.'

Then one day when the haymaking was over, and Pa took Laura into town, an old Indian entered the stores.

'Heap big snow come,' the Indian said. 'Heap big snow, big wind.'

He had said enough to make Pa move his wife and four little girls to safety in his house in town, near the shops full of supplies. But the raging blizzards came so often that there could be no trains, and it was no good being near the shops when the shops themselves ran out.

MY SIDE OF THE MOUNTAIN

JEAN GEORGE

'I am on my mountain in a tree home that people have passed without ever knowing I am here. The house is a hemlock tree six feet in diameter. I came upon it last summer and dug and burnt it out until I made a snug home in the tree.

My bed is on the right. On the left is a small fireplace with a chimney that leads the smoke out through a knothole. It snowed all day yesterday and today. It must be below zero outside, and yet I can sit here inside my tree and write with bare hands. It is the fourth of December, I think. It is eight months since I ran away from home.'

This is part of Sam Gribley's diary. Sam had escaped from his family's cramped flat in New York and his eight brothers and sisters to live on the barren farm his grandfather had owned in the Catskill Mountains. He had a pen-knife, an axe, a ball of string, and some flint and steel, and that was all.

I, JUAN DE PAREJA

ELIZABETH BORTON DE TREVINO

Juan was born into slavery early in the 17th century. He was orphaned when he was five years old, and when his mistress died she left him in her will to her nephew, who lived in Madrid. This was Don Diego Rodriguez de Silva Velazquez, the painter, who treated him gently and saw that he was healed, washed, and given new clothes.

Only two things haunted Juan – the dread that he might be sold away into crueller slavery, and the law that forbade slaves to practise the arts. In a household that lived for painting, how could Juan resist the dangerous temptation to steal colours and work secretly at what he loved best in the world.

This fascinating and unusual book won the Newbery Medal in 1966. For readers of twelve upwards.

*If you have enjoyed this book and
would like to know about others which
we publish, why not join the Puffin Club?
Membership costs 5s a year for readers living in the U.K.
or the Republic of Ireland (10s in European countries,
£1 elsewhere) and for this you will be sent the
Club magazine* Puffin Post *four times a year
and a smart badge and membership card.
You will also be able to enter all
the competitions. There is an
application form overleaf.*

APPLICATION FOR MEMBERSHIP OF
THE PUFFIN CLUB

(Write clearly in block letters)
To: THE PUFFIN CLUB SECRETARY
PENGUIN BOOKS LTD
HARMONDSWORTH
MIDDLESEX

I would like to join the Puffin Club. I enclose my membership fee for one year (see below) and would be glad if you would send me my badge and copy of *Puffin Post*.

Surname ....

Christian name(s) ....

Full Address ....

....

....

Age .... Date of Birth................................

School (name and address) ....

....

Where I buy my Puffins ....

Signature (optional) .... Date ....

Note: Membership fees for readers living in:
The U.K. or the Republic of Ireland 5s.
European countries 10s.
Elsewhere £1.